ZAK GEORGE'S
GUIDE TO A WELL-BEHAVED DOG

ZAK GEORGE'S
GUIDE TO A WELL-BEHAVED DOG

Proven Solutions to the
Most Common Training Problems
for All Ages, Breeds, and Mixes

Zak George
with Dina Roth Port

TEN SPEED PRESS
California | New York

To all the people who have helped make the
Dog Training Revolution what it is today.
Thank you for your support and for making
the world a better place for dogs.

CONTENTS

ACKNOWLEDGMENTS

My coauthor, Dina, and I would like to first thank our agent, Al Zuckerman. You have believed in us since day one, and you always work tirelessly on our behalf. We are blessed to have you in our corner. Thank you to Samantha Wekstein for all of your hard work and support. We would also like to thank our editor, Lisa Westmoreland. Your enthusiasm is infectious, and we are grateful that our book is in such skilled hands. Many thanks to designer Leona Legarte, marketing and publicity team Daniel Wikey and Lauren Kretzchmar, production manager Dan Myers, and the rest of the team at Ten Speed Press as well. And thank you to Lisa Pansini for your creative guidance and help.

From Zak

There are countless people to thank for the success the Dog Training Revolution has enjoyed over the years. However, one person in particular has really been indispensable—and that's my wife, Brianna, the most wonderful person I know.

Bree first began working with me when the Dog Training Revolution had fewer than fifty thousand subscribers on YouTube. Today we're at two million subscribers, and she has been an integral part of this explosive growth. Her passion for science and progress infuses the Dog Training Revolution with the forward-thinking principles needed to realize the goal that we and our audience share: To live in a world where people know how to intelligently raise their dogs without using outdated methods.

Bree researches the latest in scientific knowledge about dog behavior, helps produce our YouTube series, and dedicates countless hours each week to making sure that the Dog Training Revolution continues to be the gold standard in dog training. She is also the most patient, loving woman I have ever known. Thank you, Bree, for everything you do for me personally and professionally. I love you more than anything!

Our dogs Venus, Supernova, Alpha Centauri, and Indiana have certainly helped me learn *a lot* about dog behavior and dog training over the years. But, as is the case with all dogs, it was their unconditional love and my bond with them that has made me a much better person.

I can never thank my dad enough for the amazing support he's offered over the years. Also, thanks to my mom for the solid foundation she laid for me early in my life as well as for teaching me the importance of persistence and determination.

And to my coauthor Dina: Your unrelenting focus, commitment, and thoroughness to both our first book and this one has made the Dog Training Revolution more well rounded and complete. Together, you and I have written the bestselling dog training book in the United States; now, here's to launching our second book together! Thank you so much for all that you do to make our books be the best they can be.

From Dina

I would like to thank my parents for their support and for bringing Shadow, Champ, and Barkley into my life. I learned to love and appreciate animals from a very young age thanks to you.

Also, thanks to my many friends who have come to me throughout the years looking for advice on raising their dogs. Everything I've learned about dog training is from Zak! You all make me realize just how needed his books truly are.

I could never thank my husband, Larry, enough. You are my biggest champion and a true partner in every sense of the word. Thank you for all that you do for our family. I love you.

To my children, Samantha and Zachary: Thank you for being so supportive and for always telling me how proud you are of my work. You both make *me* proud every single day. I love you more than you'll ever know.

To Zak: I am so grateful to work with you and to help spread your word. You are teaching millions of people how to train their dogs in the most effective and loving way possible. I'm always happy to help you in any way I can. Thank you for being such a pleasure to work with. It has been a true honor—and a lot of fun.

And to my little loves, Baxter and Brody: You guys snuggled next to me the entire time I worked on this book. Thank you for providing the best work environment ever and for showing me just how much dogs can enrich our lives. Also, thanks for providing plenty of inspiration for this book (especially the barking chapter!). I know you're not perfect—no dog or human is—but you're perfect to me.

INTRODUCTION

Anyone who has ever had a dog knows how much these creatures can change your life for the better. You have a best friend, a constant companion, someone who's always there for you. What's better than that?

However, almost inevitably, there comes a time that your dog will drive you crazy. Maybe yours likes to stand guard by the front window and bark incessantly at every person, animal, or falling leaf he sees outside your home. Maybe he loves scratching your furniture, getting into the garbage, or digging up your yard. Or possibly you thought your fence was secure, but your dog somehow found a way out.

Of course, there are also housetraining issues, even with older dogs. You think you have made it through housetraining, and your dog is accident free. Then you step in a puddle right by the front door. Also, some dogs experience anxiety and never leave your side, especially during a thunderstorm! Others have aggression issues that can range from food guarding and leash reactivity to snapping and biting.

What's tragic is that so many of these issues are part of the reason our shelters are overflowing with unwanted dogs. Millions of people get rid of their pets, often because they just can't deal with certain disruptive behaviors. For instance, a study in the *Journal of Applied Animal Welfare Science* found that 65 percent of people who relinquished their dogs reported some behavioral issue as a reason. [1]

Sadly, hundreds of thousands of such shelter dogs are euthanized each year. [2] Others spend their lives in cages. However, there's a much better option: with a little bit of effort, you can understand why your dog acts a certain way and train him to behave the way you'd like him to. Clearly, if you're reading this book, you're taking the time to learn how to do just that. Good for you!

If you've brought home a puppy, the good news is that you're starting with a clean slate. You are teaching your dog how you want him to behave from the start. Sure, that's easier said than done. Training a puppy is a lot of work and takes a ton of time and patience. Just as you wouldn't leave a toddler unattended, you really need to do the same with a puppy. Not only can he destroy your house, but also he can get really hurt.

Even those of you who adopted an older dog from a shelter might deal with behavioral issues. First, you most likely have no idea whether your dog knows right from wrong. And your new pet's concept of "right" might actually not be right for you. For instance, maybe you don't want your dog on your furniture, but his previous family was totally okay with that. Or maybe you'd prefer your dog to bark only once when someone rings the doorbell, but he was allowed to bark as much as he liked in the past. Those are just things you'll have to reteach him. Keep in mind the whole idea that "You can't teach an old dog new tricks" is a total myth. You most certainly can.

I've seen firsthand how overwhelming it can be trying to train a dog how to behave. I've been training dogs for about sixteen years. Also, tens of millions of people use my videos on my YouTube channel, Zak George's Dog Training Revolution, to teach their dogs. Through my work as a dog trainer and educator, I have dealt with nearly every issue a person with a dog can encounter.

I've worked with so many families who bring home adorable puppies and love them more than anything. However, within time, those same people are at their wits' end because those cute puppies now weigh fifty pounds, and they're totally unmanageable on walks and jump uncontrollably on guests. I've met people who adopt dogs who seem mellow but turn out to be so high-energy once they get home that they chew everything in sight and dig up the yard because they're bored and not getting enough exercise.

I also understand the level of frustration that can go along with teaching a dog to adapt to our modern culture and rules. Like you, I've had to deal with and work through setbacks in training my own dogs as well—not just those of my clients. I've experienced what it's like to be kept up all night by a whining puppy. Trust me, I've been there. It's no fun! I've also had multiple dogs living in my home who didn't get along at first. It was tricky trying to navigate those new relationships. My first dog, Venus, was exceptional in almost every way but took an abnormal amount of time to potty train. Alpha Centauri, one of my other dogs, was very well behaved almost instantly but was a late bloomer when it came to the more advanced behaviors such as leash walking and listening at far distances. Then when Bree, my wife, and I first moved in together I had to work with her dog, Indiana, on . . . well . . . everything! Indiana is a bundle of energy and was lacking a lot of basic skills. However, she's become the best-behaved dog ever, and I was fortunate to be able to work with her. She truly made me a better teacher!

My first book, *Zak George's Dog Training Revolution: The Complete Guide to Raising the Perfect Pet with Love*, was released in 2016. That book is an all-encompassing guide to choosing, raising, and caring for your dog in every way. This one is a straight-up training guide to help you through some of the most challenging parts of teaching your dog.

This book covers issues such as excessive barking, chewing, jumping, play biting, leash pulling, hyperactivity, aggression, and more. Each chapter addresses a new topic so that you can quickly find what you need in the book when issues arise. You'll learn why dogs behave in ways we don't exactly prefer, what you can do to prevent such undesirable behaviors, and how to encourage good behaviors instead!

It has been so humbling and exciting to commit my life to something I absolutely love: working with dogs and sharing what I've learned with other people. For instance, I've learned that most people new to dogs and training them underestimate just how smart and capable dogs are. I've also realized that nothing sets you up for success better than always making sure that your relationship with your dog is prioritized in all phases of training. I spent years performing with my dogs in stunt dog shows around America. I learned quickly that if I expected my dogs to go out there and perform some of the most elaborate tricks and stunts imaginable, then I needed to have a very strong bond and connection with them. I've also found that even when you're just teaching your dog the basic skills, the same is true.

That doesn't mean *all* types of training are effective or even humane. Sadly, dog training is one of those fields that is the Wild West in many ways. With no regulations, there are countless approaches that people use out there. In this era where people often demand fast, even instant results, we've seen the continued use of electric shock collars—which, by the way, have been banned in England, Denmark, Sweden, Switzerland, Germany, and many other countries.[3] We've also seen the use of choke and prong collars.

All three of these devices are specifically engineered to be highly unpleasant, even painful, to dogs. And even though they may appear to "work" short term, they do nothing to promote a bond between you and your dog. Plus, a dog is bound to revert to his old behaviors once the collar comes off. That's not teaching—it's just a very shallow way to communicate with a highly intelligent animal. These tools have absolutely no place in the dog training world.

I've also heard trainers use the word *dominance* as a blanket term to explain every unwanted dog behavior under the sun. They use this to justify harsh, physical methods that defeat a dog but do nothing to teach or happily motivate a dog. There is a mountain of science that shows such methods—ranging from yelling at your dog, rolling him onto his back, and staring him down to using painful collars or hurting him physically in any other way—are ineffective and do more harm than good.[4] You deserve better advice than this! I'll show you what to do without intimidation, force, or other outdated methods.

Lastly, I've discovered that every dog learns differently. Authentic teaching comes about through commitment, patience, and understanding that your dog is as much an individual as any human. No two dogs are the same. Keep this front of mind. Also, remember that, as with almost everything, gimmicks and quick fixes are not likely to give you the results you want. However, hard work and commitment will. Of course, you first need to know what to do. And that's precisely what this book—along with my free videos on YouTube—will show you. Whatever your issue is with your dog, we'll fix it or at least greatly improve it together. Let's get started!

PART I

THE BASICS

CHAPTER 1

TEN ESSENTIALS FOR A WELL-BEHAVED DOG

Having worked with so many dogs over the years, I can tell you that every single one of them is a unique individual. And when it comes to training, each one requires a tailored approach. The dog you had growing up or at any time in the past is different from the one you have now.

In fact, if I could change one thing about how people view teaching dogs, it would be this very thing. Too often, we have the tendency to think about dogs as though they are computers simply needing to be programmed. Many people believe that you can train every dog the same way. That's simply not true. Others think there's one set of training principles for German Shepherds, one for Labradors, one for Cocker Spaniels, and so on. This, too, is incorrect, but even some of my own colleagues fall victim to these broad stereotypes.

I won't focus on teaching you quick fixes or on getting you results with shallow or gimmicky dog training advice. Instead, I *will* offer you sound advice that can help you train your dog to her full potential.

Throughout this book, I will help you through the most common issues people face with their dogs. And I will address each topic individually, step by step. However, it's critical to know that there are fundamentals everyone needs to consider when training dogs—no matter *what* you're teaching.

As you try to work through issues ranging from leash pulling, barking, and jumping up to hyperactivity, anxiety, and aggressive behaviors, make sure you first address the points I cover in this chapter. The following ten basic concepts are nonnegotiable for every dog if you hope to have great results.

1. MAKE YOUR RELATIONSHIP TOP PRIORITY

Think about why you got a dog to begin with. It was probably because you wanted a loyal, loving companion who could totally enrich your life, right? Almost nobody gets a dog because they want an unemotional animal who acts like a robot. And that's a great thing!

If you were creating a building that you cared about, you would make sure that the foundation of that structure was solid, that every brick was in place, and that there were no weak points so that everything built on top of it would be solid, too. Well, the relationship you have with your dog is also critical. When it comes to training, it's the foundation that everything else is built on. Never compromise it. In fact, make your bond the centerpiece of all training moving forward. If you don't, then it's unrealistic to expect meaningful results.

Too often people get dogs and they hold them to unrealistic, rigid standards immediately. I get it! You want your dog to listen right from the beginning—and that's fine. However, you've really got to choose your battles with a new dog. The beginning is such a crucial time to establish trust and love, and this should take precedence over everything else.

See, it's easy to get into a trap of constantly correcting a dog, particularly a brand-new puppy or a dog straight out of a shelter. However, at first, I just want you to mostly work on your bond with your dog. That's because effective training requires you to have mutually earned trust between the two of you. That takes time. So be tolerant and focus on really connecting with your dog over those first few weeks (regardless of her age). The relationship you build will be the cornerstone for *everything*.

The most epic dog I've ever known was my dog Venus. Yes, I am biased, but really . . . she was incredible. She was the first dog who, as an adult, I committed to teaching at a high level. At first, I got her because I wanted a Frisbee dog and a companion. Well, I certainly got those two things and so much more. Venus completely changed my life. She showed me that not only are dogs capable of much more than I had ever thought possible, but they also have the immense capacity to love and enrich our lives in ways that are difficult to put into words. Surely anyone who has ever loved a dog will relate. Yes, Venus excelled at training, and she was an incredible pupil. But looking back at her life in its totality now, I understand that the bond we had and the love we had for one another means far more than all of her accomplishments combined.

What if you feel that you've already been too hard on your dog? Is it too late to establish a better relationship? The good news is that dogs are great at appreciating life in the moment. They don't hold grudges. If you take your time and remain tolerant and understanding from now on, you can still develop a strong relationship.

So how do you go about bonding with your dog? First, know that this is such a personal thing—it really depends on the dog. However, in my experience, I've found that if you can get your dog playing with you, you will be on the right track toward building a tight bond.

Researchers have discovered that dogs enjoy exercise in a way that's similar to humans. For example, a study in the *Journal of Experimental Biology* found that dogs can actually experience a "runner's high." [1] So, pair that with the fact that dogs historically love working with and just being with humans, and you'll find that some playtime together can do wonders for your relationship.

Maybe your dog is more mellow. Maybe she's more reserved and just not into vigorous play. That's okay too! Find what does make your dog happy and focus on that. Some dogs love being petted affectionately. Others enjoy going for a stroll around the block and taking in all of the great smells, sounds, and sights. Others just love snuggling next to you on the couch. What's critical is that you take advantage of every opportunity to make sure that your dog knows she can count on you to make her happy.

Of course, to bond with your dog and to teach her that she can trust you, you also have to be a good pet parent in other ways. For instance, feeding your dog healthy food, making sure she gets plenty of water, taking her for regular vet visits, and giving her basic affection are critical. The same goes for learning your dog's body language and understanding when she's happy, sad, scared, or in pain. I think you'll find that these things become somewhat intuitive as you get to know your dog!

Every person and every dog is different, and building a relationship with your dog is a unique process. However, remember that just as you easily fell in love with your dog, she can easily fall in love with you, too: a study published in *Science* found that when humans and their dogs simply look into one another's eyes, they experience the same boost in oxytocin—the feel-good hormone—as mothers and infants do.[2] In other words, with a little bit of effort on your part, you can have a strong bond with your pet that lasts for years to come.

2. FOCUS ON ENERGY LEVEL, NOT BREED

Many people think that the best way to describe a dog's personality is by breed. However, there is so much more to dogs than their breeds. Sure, it makes sense to consider or rule out specific breeds because of physical characteristics such as size and shedding. However, when it comes to training a dog (and choosing one, for that matter), the dog's breed is one of the last things I tell people to consider.

People often focus so much on breed stereotypes that they're then upset when their pet doesn't live up to those expectations. Yet, if you looked at ten dogs from the same breed, you might notice they have ten very different personalities. Trust me—I lived with three Border Collies at one point, and while they did share some similarities like their love for playing Frisbee, they couldn't have been more different from one another. For instance, Venus was a little standoffish to other people and dogs and not a big snuggler. But Supernova? That dog would have literally attached himself to me 24/7 if he could.

So, what should you focus on instead of breed when developing your training strategy? Focus on your dog's energy level and individual personality (all of her quirks included!). Understanding your dog's energy level can also help you get to the root of why she might be having behavioral issues. For example, if a dog doesn't have an outlet for releasing all of her energy, then she just might use that energy to chew up your shoes or dig up your yard. So, let's go over the three basic categories of energy levels and what they mean.

Energy Level 1: Low

Level one dogs are typically calm, laid-back couch potatoes. They're happy just to take a few short walks with you, and then they'll basically chill out for the rest of the day. Don't expect a level one dog to play vigorously for long periods of time (or at all in some cases). Most level one dogs won't be super-motivated to learn very advanced or athletic tasks. This doesn't mean they are less intelligent; they are just more relaxed. They also tend to be naturally well behaved—for instance, they don't typically have the energy to, say, chew up everything in your house or pull you down the street on walks. They'd rather just take it easy.

Energy Level 2: Moderate

Level two dogs have more physical and mental stamina than level one dogs. A level two dog might get *really* excited when you walk in the door, but after a few minutes she calms down without much encouragement from you. These dogs can have substantial bursts of energy, and they generally require fairly significant exercise to realize their true potential. They are great for people who want to have a hands-on role in teaching their dogs but don't want exercising their dogs to completely take over their lives. Level two dogs can learn a variety of advanced tasks, but they are not likely to excel at really extreme athletic endeavors.

Energy Level 3: High

Now, let's talk about those super–high-energy dogs—you know, the ones that can play all day and night! The dogs who jump like crazy or constantly bring you toys to play fetch or tug with are classic level three dogs. Let me let you in on a big secret: in general, the more energy a dog has, the more teachable she is. However, these dogs are *not* for the casual pet parent as they tend to be high maintenance—*very* high maintenance!

You have to dedicate a lot of time to making sure these dogs get plenty of mental and physical exercise. If you don't, all that pent-up energy will almost certainly lead to excessive hyperactivity and destructive behaviors. These dogs virtually always require very significant exercise before each training lesson. It seems that they can't focus until they release that excess energy. Also, the kind of exercise matters. Roaming in your yard, going for a walk, or playing with other dogs usually isn't good enough. As I mentioned earlier in this chapter, dogs are most satisfied when they exercise by interacting directly with you.

Yes, I'm making a lot of generalizations here, and there are no doubt exceptions out there. In all likelihood, your dog is somewhere between these categories. For example, your dog could be a level 1.3 or a 2.5. It's a spectrum. Bottom line: Understanding your dog's energy level is a great way to get a general idea of how much time and effort she's going to require from you. It's the *most* important factor to consider when you approach training her.

Remember, the majority of dogs with "behavior problems" are higher-energy dogs because people have greatly underestimated the level of regular training and activity these dogs require. Also, keep in mind that a dog maintains her energy level for a good portion of her life. So, if you have a rambunctious puppy, chances are she's going to stay rambunctious for most of her life. Don't expect her to settle down after a couple of years.

3. UNDERSTAND THE IMPORTANCE OF EXERCISE IN TRAINING

Structured exercise is, by far, the number one piece of advice I give as a dog trainer. In fact, 90 percent of unwanted behaviors are due to the fact that your dog is bored and not getting the physical and mental stimulation she needs (especially those moderate- to high-energy dogs!). If your dog tends to jump on people often or behave frantically when excited, then regular exercise, usually early in the day, is the single most important thing that is likely to make a difference.

Exercise is also a tremendous way to get traction on improving lots of behavioral issues, including those relating to anxiety and aggression. A study in Finland found that the daily amount of exercise was the largest factor affecting whether or not a dog had separation anxiety or noise sensitivity.[3] Also, dogs who took shorter walks were more likely to be fearful than those who took longer walks. Another survey by researchers from Bristol University in the United Kingdom found that the more that people play with their dogs, the fewer behavioral issues (such as whining, jumping up, and not coming when called) their pets have.[4]

Let's also examine why exercise is so critical from a *training* perspective. Dogs were selectively bred over thousands of years for one common purpose: to work with, cooperate with, and take direction from people. The relationship between people and dogs is a symbiotic one, and we have a rich history of working together in many ways. A common trait selected for many of these dogs was energy—and lots of it! The more stamina and endurance dogs had for those long work days, the more valuable they were to us.

Something has changed though. The very nature of the way we work very seldom requires a dog's assistance these days. Many of us go to work during the day, and our dogs are left home with little to do. Dogs' genetics haven't changed that much, so many of them still have a natural desire to work with and play with people.

Fortunately, there is something relatively easy we can do to satisfy the mental and physical needs for those dogs: make sure your dog gets enough exercise *with* you. The fastest, easiest way to do that is to teach your dog fetch. I cover how to teach fetch on page 149, chapter 17, but for now, understand that fetch, as I define it, is where your dog chases a toy, picks it up immediately, promptly returns the toy in a straight line, drops it promptly when asked, and eagerly awaits the next throw.

The thrill of chasing an item, coupled with working directly with a human, satisfies many of those traits we selected for in the past, such as traits used in hunting. Also, the beautiful thing about fetch is that it allows your dog to get tons of energy out without requiring a lot of your time or physical exertion. A proper game of fetch does takes time to teach though: it's normal for it to take a few months to really perfect. However, it's definitely worth the effort.

Of course, there are some dogs who are just not into fetch. Usually, these are the level one dogs as well as some level two dogs. For these dogs, hikes or long walks may suffice. I'd also encourage you to be creative about providing exercise to your dog—for instance, you might want to look into various dog sports and other activities that she may enjoy. I will remind you throughout this book that vigorous, age-appropriate exercise may be required with many dogs just prior to training them. In order for your dog to retain new concepts and behaviors, you must be fair to her and give her an outlet for her natural energy first. And remember, if a dog is exhibiting rambunctious, destructive, or anxious behaviors, my first suggestion is usually to make sure she's getting enough exercise. There's more about that in the next chapter.

When Should I Exercise My Dog?

When you exercise your dog matters a great deal. I highly recommend doing so early in the day. Think about it: when is a dog likely to be most charged up and energetic? After getting a good night's sleep! By exercising your dog early in the day, you are getting lots of her energy out, which further encourages her to mellow out afterward. Many dogs will also require multiple exercise sessions throughout the day. You may need to exercise yours before work, at lunch, and just before bed, for instance.

How Do I Determine Age-Appropriate Exercise?

How much exercise is okay for a dog? This really depends on a variety of factors, such as your dog's fitness level, genetics, and sometimes breed (as in the case of brachycephalic dogs—those with shortened noses and flat faces such as Pugs and Shih Tzus). One of the most important things to consider is your dog's age. Here's what you need to know.

PUPPIES

When it comes to exercise, you have to be careful with puppies because their growth plates—the areas of soft cartilage tissue found at the end of a young dog's long bones—are still soft, open, and vulnerable to injuries. If an injury *does* occur, your dog's growth can be stunted. The growth plates eventually get thinner and close between one and two years, depending on your dog. It's important to be very conservative with exercise until this happens.

While your vet can help you determine how much exercise is appropriate for your puppy, a general rule of thumb is five minutes of exercise at a time, up to two times a day, for every one month of age. So, if your puppy is two months old, she can exercise for ten minutes at a time, up to twice per day. And if your puppy is six months old, she can exercise for thirty minutes at a time, up to twice per day.

What kind of exercise can you do with your puppy while you're waiting for her to grow up? The safest type of exercise for young puppies are short walks and free play, which is basically letting them do their own thing. Puppies are pretty good at staying active and knowing their limits. So, when your puppy decides it's time to take a break, let her!

That being said, puppies can occasionally get a little too crazy with their play. If you notice yours doing crazy flips and somersaults, intervene and let her calm down for a bit before she resumes playing. Also, prevent her from jumping off furniture. That could really hurt her growing bones. When you're playing with a young dog, be careful to keep her close to the ground by dragging or rolling toys instead of throwing them. And when you're tugging, make sure to tug gently and parallel with the ground, not upward.

OLDER DOGS

Of course, once your dog is no longer a puppy, she can handle a lot more exercise! Knowing how much to exercise your dog, especially if she's energetic, is an essential part of raising her.

First, keep in mind that some breeds or types of dogs need extra consideration when it comes to exercise limits, so do your research on your dog's breed or mix if you know it. For instance, brachycephalic dogs can struggle with breathing if overexercised. Always consult with your vet about the amount of exercise that might be appropriate for your dog based on her overall size, age, breed, and individual health.

In general, most high-energy full-grown dogs require forty-five minutes to one hour of exercise per day, four to five days a week. And that's if you're playing fetch or another intense activity that involves participation from you. If you're just walking your high-energy dog, then she might require a walk that's two hours or longer. Moderate- to lower-energy dogs may require less than that—for them, walking twenty to thirty minutes or less and doing some basic training is a great way to exercise them.

If you have a high-energy dog and are looking for other options, you may want to take up more formal activities like Frisbee, agility, dock diving, or flyball. Dog sports are a fantastic way to fulfill a dog mentally and physically. Ask your vet and trusted friends with dogs for suggestions on where to find such activities in your area.

4. TEACH FROM THE INSIDE OUT

The most fundamental point to my training advice is this: teach your dog from the inside out. *Inside-out training* means you are teaching your dog to behave in a certain way because she wants to. *Outside-in training* means you are *making* your dog behave a certain way.

This is where my training advice diverges from some of what you've likely heard about training dogs. It's the antithesis of traditional training. Those metal training collars that restrict around your dog's throat have long been the go-to tools of many trainers—and they are often at the center of outside-in training. The disturbing trend of electric shock collars is a continuation of this flawed approach.

I get that there's something intuitive about "correcting" a dog when she behaves less than ideally. If she pulls on a leash, then providing a sudden, swift pop of the collar can show your dog that things can be very unpleasant when she walks a little too fast. Or if she jumps, a quick knee to the chest will stop her from doing it. It's not that these approaches won't discourage unwanted behaviors, it's just that there's a more reliable, effective, and ethical way to teach dogs than by constantly correcting them.

First and most important, outside-in training doesn't help foster a strong, loving relationship with your dog (if anything, the opposite can be true). Also, keep in mind that forcing a dog to do something doesn't help her think for herself and learn the right way to behave. In fact, when choke or shock collars are removed, the majority of dogs revert to their old behaviors, further illustrating that actual, deep learning has not occurred. Instead, the dog has simply learned to avoid pain or discomfort when those training collars are on. My job is to show you how to get your dog listening to you regardless of what collar she's wearing.

The same thing is true even if you use something as seemingly benign as an anxiety vest to help your dog stay calm during a thunderstorm. You're only addressing the symptom, not the cause. Without that vest, your dog will still be nervous. Wouldn't it be better to actually help her mitigate or even eliminate her fear of thunder and other loud noises altogether? Or say your dog loves to chew up your shoes. Sure, you can spray all of your shoes with a bitter spray. However, doesn't it make more sense to actually teach your dog not to chew such items in the first place? I'll show you how to address the causes of many issues such as anxiety and chewing so you don't have to rely on these quick-but-temporary fixes.

Another important point: When you rely on a strategy of correcting a dog after she does something you don't like, you are too late. In fact, it's probably ten times more difficult to break a bad habit than it is to prevent establishing one in the first place. I realize that this is tough to understand initially. It's probably the biggest hurdle I face when teaching people how to teach their dogs. I mean, how are you supposed to prevent a jumping, lunging dog from doing these things? If she doesn't learn by being corrected, then how is she ever supposed to learn at all? I'll answer these questions in depth throughout this book.

For now, however, know that when you motivate your dog to want to listen to you rather than physically making her behave a certain way, you are on the road to actually teaching your dog. Most dogs will sit for a treat, right? This is a good example of showing your dog what you want and providing a great outcome rather than pushing her butt down on the ground if she doesn't do it. It's up to you show your dog how to voluntarily do things you wish.

Think about teaching young children how to do multiplication. You must take the time to sit with them, work through the problems, and be patient. You can't do it passively, and you can't force them to think or understand. And, of course, if you do their math homework for them, then they really won't learn a thing!

It's similar with dogs and training. When you reward your dog with treats, playtime, and lots of praise and affection, your dog is going to *want* to continue the behavior that got her all those awesome things. If you've ever had a particular passion such as sports, music, or any hobby or interest, you'll probably recall that you found lots of joy in it—so much so, that you were willing to go out of your way to participate in it. So, you'll need to cater to the things your dog loves in order to achieve long-lasting, authentic results in your training.

One more note: There will be times when you need to pick up your dog or escort her away from, say, a dangerous situation, such as when she encounters another dog exhibiting aggressive behaviors. Or if your dog freezes up on the leash and doesn't budge during a walk, you might have to pick her up, if possible, and place her on the grass so she can go potty (and then schedule dedicated training sessions to work on this issue, of course). I don't view this as outside-in training as much as I consider it management, which I explain in depth on page 26 in this chapter. I'm not assuming that physically removing your dog from a situation or placing her in one actually teaches her anything. Instead, it's just a way to correct yourself when you've inadvertently put your dog in a sticky situation or one she just isn't ready for yet.

5. CONTROL THE ENVIRONMENT

The most common mistake made by people with new dogs is giving them too much freedom too early. Not controlling your dog's environment well is the greatest contributing factor to allowing the establishment of undesirable habits. In other words, if you want your dog to avoid picking up bad habits, relentlessly control where she can and can't go and what she has access to for the first year of training at least (especially for puppies and untrained older dogs).

Controlling a dog's environment is also key in resolving unwanted behaviors like barking. Let's say your dog barks at everyone and everything that walks in front of your house. If you rely on redirecting her attention to you *after* she has started barking, then this means you'll have to go to where she is in the house (as she continues to bark for a few more seconds, further establishing the unwanted behavior) and then redirect her attention to you. Whereas, if you are *right* there to get her attention on you immediately when someone walks past your house, you can then reward her for ideal behavior before the barking even starts.

The best way to keep control of your dog is by having her attached to you with a leash as often as possible. I'll be honest, too few people take my advice on this. They think they can bypass this step, but that's not advisable for the majority of dogs. I'm not talking about having your dog on leash only when outside of the house. I want you to attach her to you often when inside the house, too.

By having your dog attached to your belt loop or otherwise tied to you, not only do you prevent her from chewing on furniture or shoes, jumping all over small children, and bolting out of the front door, but you are also in an ideal position to provide feedback to let your dog know when you *like* her behavior. Also, when your dog does perform less than ideally, you are right there to interrupt the actions you don't like and show her what you'd prefer her to do instead. Whenever you are at home and able to attach your dog to you, do it.

Of course, you can't always supervise your dog this thoroughly. You have to work, run errands, and relax sometimes. In these cases, it's critical that you make sure that you have your dog in a controlled setting where she can't tear up your belongings, pee on the floor, or acquire other bad habits. Crates are an excellent way to keep dogs safe for short periods of time. When introducing a crate, proceed slowly and at your dog's pace. Lots of dogs learn to love their crate as it's their own special place. Check out my various YouTube videos on how to introduce a dog to her crate, such as *How to Potty Train Your Puppy Easily! Everything You Need to Know!*

However, some dogs will never like staying in a crate. Also, even if your dog loves her crate, she shouldn't spend more than four hours in it at a time (or less depending on her age). That's why it's important to have other options for keeping your dog's environment controlled while you're out of the house or preoccupied at home. For instance, you might want to puppy proof a bathroom or other area in the house so that your dog has a bit more room while you're away. Indoor exercise pens and baby/puppy gates are another great way for your dog to have additional room while being kept safe.

6. KNOW YOUR DOG'S CURRENCY

We all love incentives. Tell a child that you'll take her for ice cream or buy her a toy if she makes her bed every morning, and you can bet that she'll tuck those sheets in tight. Of course, the reverse is true. If you tell a kid she can't watch TV or have a friend over if she doesn't eat her veggies, she'll more likely try a bite of something green.

Well, dogs are the same as humans in this respect. They are more likely to repeat an action, like sit, when the outcome is favorable (say, you give them a treat). In the training world, this is called *reinforcement*. On the flip side, dogs are less likely to repeat a behavior when the outcome is unfavorable to them. We refer to this unfavorable outcome as *punishment*.

Note that when dog trainers and behaviorists refer to punishment, they might mean anything that is viewed as unpleasant to a dog. In our case, we limit unpleasant outcomes to withholding something they want or denying access to a particular environment. For example, provided you've taught your dog to sit, if you ask her to do so and she doesn't, you now need to provide an undesired but humane consequence. In this case, you might withhold a treat or not let her run into the backyard until she first holds a ten-second sit.

I know you've probably come across trainers who promote physical punishment. When their dogs have accidents in the house, they rub their pets' noses in it. They yell at their dogs and flip them on their backs in what's called an "alpha roll." They use the choke, prong, or electric collars I mentioned earlier. Please don't do any of these things!

Remember that physical punishment is the shallowest form of punishing a dog. It's not only unnecessary and ineffective, but it can also destroy your bond with your dog, which, as I mentioned earlier in this chapter, is the cornerstone of training.

While you should always praise your dog with a "Good girl!" or a similar phrase when she does something you like, praise by itself is not usually enough to encourage long-term repeated behavior in the first several months of training. You've got to use your dog's currency. In fact, whether reinforcing behaviors you do like or punishing behaviors you don't, you'll need to use your dog's currency very consistently throughout her training.

What is currency? There are three main types: food and play are the most common, while the third type of currency is environment. I'll walk you through all three options.

Food

Virtually all dogs are motivated by food, provided that you are attempting to train them in a situation that they are used to and with food that they love. When using food for primary training sessions, use a high-value food reward almost exclusively. Think of it like a one dollar bill. A good choice is usually plain, boiled chicken, turkey, or something extra-special like that. It's essential that your dog loves the currency, not just like it.

However, that doesn't mean she gets a huge piece of chicken every time she does something good. When using treats, it's quality, not quantity, that's important. Plus, the last thing you want is your dog getting too full (or overweight!). So, the size of food rewards should be between the size of a grain of rice and a pea. This also goes a long way toward setting up "jackpot" rewards that you can use when your dog really breaks new ground in training. In other words, sometimes when teaching dogs, we have to supply rapid-fire treats, one after the other. You can't do that if the currency is too large.

Traditional dog treats have their place in training, too. Think of their value as being a quarter. Dog treats are convenient to have readily available throughout the house, in your car, or in your pocket or purse so that you can quickly reward your dog in those unexpected secondary training sessions. Stick with soft ones, which are usually more palatable and desirable to dogs than dry ones (freeze-dried meat treats are an exception). Plus, they're easy to break up into small pieces, which you should still do. Almost all commercial dog treats are way too big to be given at once for training purposes.

You can use bits of kibble or dry treats during training on occasion, too. However, they are equivalent to a penny. Use these sparingly. Remember, the currency has to really excite your dog, and a bit of kibble or a dry treat isn't going to do the trick in the same way a piece of meat will. I generally do not advise using kibble or dry treats for training on a regular basis.

Play

Sure, food motivates a lot of dogs, but many people overlook play as a potential currency, too. However, for a huge percentage of dogs— especially those with a lot of energy—some type of play is the *ultimate* currency. The most common examples of play as a currency are three- to ten-second games of tug-of-war and fetch. That's right, sometimes a simple toss of a ball just a few feet is very intoxicating and motivating for dogs. A lot of dogs will do anything for even the most insignificant toss of a toy. My dogs were even more driven by that than by food! In fact, I taught them almost exclusively with play as a currency, and they would even abandon their food at mealtime if they simply caught a glimpse of me picking up their ball. It was quite hilarious, actually.

So how do you use play as currency exactly? For many dogs, playing with you in a way that allows them to run, chase, and tug is highly fulfilling. For example, if your dog does something that you ask, go ahead and reward her with a few seconds of tug-of-war or a short toss of a ball (provided you've taught this!). If your dog doesn't listen to a request, you can simply withhold the fun game until she does.

I include a detailed description of tug-of-war on page 79, chapter 7, and one of fetch on page 149, chapter 17. Also, I know that not all dogs respond equally to tug-of-war and fetch as a currency. However, it's always worth a try since using play as a currency can make all the difference in your dog's willingness to keep learning and training.

A NOTE ON INTERMITTENT REINFORCEMENT

Some of you might wonder how effective your training will be if you reward your dog all of the time. It's true that I advise rewarding very often in the early stages of training. However, as training goes on, and your dog begins to reliably listen with fairly heavy rewarding, you should start focusing on rewarding randomly, maybe 75 percent of the time at first, then 40 percent, then 90 percent, and then 20 percent. Use your own percentages—just keep it random. Intermittent reinforcement is highly effective when teaching because it keeps your dog guessing. Ultimately, you might only give your dog her currency every ten times or even every thirty. You can determine how often based on how reliably your dog is listening without her currency. There's more on this on page 195, chapter 22.

Environment

Along with food and playtime, you can use your dog's environment as currency. Truthfully, you probably won't need to do this as often as you'd use the other methods, but it can still be quite effective at times. For example, when teaching your dog to stay at a doorway leading to the outside, she might be *very* excited to get out in the yard and start smelling around. So not letting her run into the yard until she's held a ten-second stay can be a significant motivator. Dogs are usually eager to comply if it means they get to go outside! Another example: When your dog is pulling on her leash, stopping and waiting for a compliant "look at me" and then rewarding her by continuing the walk can be an additional way to reinforce good behavior. On the flip side, bringing the walk to a stop is one way to provide an undesired outcome for your dog when she pulls. You're basically saying to her, "We can walk, but it has to be on my terms." Eventually, after a lot of repetition, this lesson starts to sink in.

7. MAKE THE MOST OF PRIMARY AND SECONDARY TRAINING SESSIONS

There are two main types of training sessions: primary and secondary. Understanding the importance of both types of sessions is vital to teaching a dog to listen to you in virtually every setting. Remember, always make sure you have your dog's currency available during these sessions. Here's a breakdown of each.

Primary Training

Primary training sessions are for when you are teaching something new to your dog. In a primary lesson, you are 100 percent focused on teaching your dog something specific in a very deliberate, slow manner. Take "sit," for example. Here, you are using your dog's currency to slowly lure her into the "sit" position. (See page 46, chapter 3, for a refresher on this skill). You are not asking her to learn this concept around tons of distractions or other dogs. Nor are you requiring that she snap into a "sit," like a soldier, on the first request. Instead, you are setting up time to patiently teach your dog the skill, just like you'd patiently teach a young child how to read or write.

Primary lessons are where you should introduce and practice concepts. Always plan and conduct them in places where you have virtually total control of the environment, such as in your house or fenced yard. Primary lessons should also always occur in environments where your dog is likely to maintain her focus on you. In other words, make sure the distractions, scents, sounds, and sights at the place where you're teaching are not too overwhelming for your dog at her current skill level. This might mean your living room if your dog is new to training, but it can also mean a busy park if you've worked up to training in such a place with your dog.

SURPRISE PRIMARY TRAINING

The next level of primary training is *surprise primary training sessions.* That's when you attempt to introduce variables that mimic real-life distractions. These are still planned on your end, but your dog should have no notice that a training session is about to occur. For example, say your dog is hanging out next to you while you cook. You might intentionally drop a carrot on the floor and ask your dog to "leave it." From your perspective, you've thought about the training drill that's about to happen. You are prepared to promptly request that your dog leave the carrot alone a second before it hits the ground. You're prepared to give your dog a treat if she complies, and you're ready to cover the carrot or pick it up if your dog seems to ignore your request.

However, from your dog's perspective, she has no idea what's coming. This element of surprise is essential for dogs who have mastered the basic primary sessions. See, a huge part of training a dog to behave well is to make sure that she behaves well in *all* situations, not just when she's totally prepared for a training session. Building basic impulse control takes extensive practice with most dogs. It's not that difficult, but you have to do it often and in varied ways for months.

Secondary Training

Secondary training sessions are totally unplanned. They require you to drop what you are doing to show your dog how to behave in the moment that she is misbehaving. This is the real deal!

The good news is that if you did plenty of surprise primary training sessions, you should be fine. See, that's why those sessions are so critical. Since they imitate things that might happen in real life—say, you ask a friend to knock on your front door or you purposefully set a turkey sandwich out on the counter—your dog is likely to be much more successful when those things *actually* occur.

Unfortunately, most people focus only on the first kind of structured primary sessions I addressed in this section, but they skip the surprise ones. Then, they're shocked that their dog can't focus when they're training them in a real-life, secondary session. Without those surprise sessions under her belt, your dog likely won't know how to react appropriately.

So, what do you do in secondary training sessions? Most importantly, get your dog's attention on you as soon as possible and reward her with her currency if she complies. For example, say you're on your daily walk with your dog and she suddenly spots another dog or cat down the street. If your dog starts to lunge and bark, then create distance between your dog and the distraction until your dog is compliant. Reward her when she is. Or say you're home and an unexpected guest suddenly knocks on your front door. If your dog starts barking and running toward the door, then take the time to get your dog's attention on you and reward for quiet behavior, even if it's minimal at first.

There may well be times when your dog is too distracted to focus on you during a secondary training session. In those cases, the key is to simply manage your dog by getting away from the thing that's setting her off. Then, take a step back and, when you have time, set up primary training sessions to better prepare your dog.

So, if your dog starts regularly chasing bicycles when surprised by one, make it a point to do some primary training with your dog on leash in the presence of bikes at your local park where you can control the distance between your dog and the bikes. Your goal would be to desensitize her to bikes during the primary sessions so she won't be as surprised or reactive to them. (There's much more on desensitization in the next section and throughout the book.) In other words, when you cannot get your dog's focus in a secondary session, you have to do more primary training and surprise primary training.

I know that you'll have many questions about how to conduct these various types of training sessions in specific instances. Throughout this book, I'll give you examples of how to implement primary, surprise primary, and secondary training sessions to resolve all sorts of behavior problems. If you practice all three types of lessons in all aspects of your training, you most certainly will have a dog who listens to you reliably.

8. LEARN THE THREE CRITICAL BEHAVIOR MODIFICATION TECHNIQUES

You'll notice that there's a basic framework that I apply when addressing many behavior problems: management, desensitization, and conditioning or counterconditioning. These behavior modification techniques go hand in hand, and I'll explain often and throughout the book how to achieve progress with this formula! Here's a breakdown of each.

1. Management

Management is really key with dog training—and, quite honestly, this is where most people make mistakes. What I mean by *management* is controlling your dog's environment—as described earlier in this chapter—and, in the case of anxiety and fear, keeping your dog from being overwhelmed in a certain situation. For example, your dog cannot jump on guests if she is on leash and several feet away from your guests. She can't chew your shoes or dig up your yard if she doesn't have unsupervised access to either. She can't experience overwhelming fear of, say, your vacuum cleaner if you don't turn it on next to her.

Management also means using the environment itself to intentionally train at your dog's current level of ability. Maybe your dog is great when you ask for a "look at me" when she's thirty yards away from a particular distraction, but perhaps she doesn't listen at ten yards away. By managing the intensity of various distractions, you are putting your dog in a better position to succeed.

Stopping all unwanted behaviors first requires you to bring the behavior to a stop. You shouldn't do this by punishing or forcefully making your dog stop doing something undesired. Instead, you can be one step ahead of her and prevent very predictable behaviors, like jumping, from occurring in the first place. So, if your dog is continually doing things that you wish she wouldn't, ask yourself how well you are managing her surroundings. I bet you'll find that you could probably control her environment a bit better.

Of course, while management is critical in dog training, it's only part of the equation. Along with making sure your dog doesn't engage in undesirable behaviors, you also need to teach her the correct ones. That's what this book is all about!

2. Desensitization

Many common behavioral issues—especially those related to anxiety and fear—are a result of a dog being unfamiliar with something. For instance, many dogs might bark at other dogs or people in public because they are unfamiliar with those dogs and people. Or they may freeze up on a leash because they're not used to a new park. Very often, a dog simply needs to get familiar with something to then become civilized around it! *Desensitization* lets you carefully expose your pet to whatever is causing her anxiety or fear at a level that's not too overwhelming for her.

We can all relate to this. Think about the first day of school when you were a kid. Maybe you were a little nervous (or *very* nervous as was the case for me!). You didn't yet know who would be in your class, what your teacher was going to be like, or how hard the curriculum was going to be. But sure enough, after a few days or weeks, those emotions were tempered, and you probably relaxed a bit. You were, in fact, less sensitive as those unknowns became familiar and you adapted and adjusted to them.

It's the same way for dogs. A dog might be scared of a new place or person. However, after spending time in that new place or with that new person without anything bad happening, she might start to realize, "Hey! I'm okay. There's nothing to be nervous about." In other words, frequent, safe, planned exposure to things that cause dogs to become nervous or fearful should be a powerful part of your training strategy.

3. Conditioning and Counterconditioning

When we talk about *conditioning* a dog in dog training, we simply mean getting your dog to have a favorable association with something. For example, when you ask your dog to sit and then give her a treat when she does, your dog learns, "Wow, I complied with that request and got something awesome as a result." This causes her to become conditioned to sitting more reliably when you ask her to sit in the future.

When we talk about *counterconditioning*, we mean that we are changing an existing association to a particular stimulus. Let's say that a dog is nervous around strangers. Maybe she has had bad experiences with new people, or she simply lacks exposure to people. Either way, she has a response to strangers that you'd like to change.

If you begin to offer amazing treats to your dog in the presence of strangers, then your dog might stop thinking, "I'm terrified of strangers!" and start thinking, "I love strangers because I often get something great when I'm around them." Of course, I'm oversimplifying a bit here to make my point, but this concept is critical in training. So, throughout the book, I'll give specifics on how to countercondition your dog to things to which she already has an undesired response.

Here's another example: a lot of the dogs I film videos with are nervous in my studio at first because it's a new place—and many dogs become uneasy in new places. So, if a dog seems apprehensive, I immediately initiate counterconditioning measures and offer her small bits of chicken or a super-fun squeaky toy to play with. With *really* nervous dogs, I'll also encourage them to relax and let their people provide subtle comfort in the hope that this may reassure them. In other words, I'll do what I can to change the dog's mind-set from something like, "This place is making me nervous" to "This place is actually pretty awesome."

9. PRACTICE CONSISTENCY

One of the most essential aspects of dog training is extreme consistency. I can't stress this enough! When you commit to asking your dog to, say, come when called, stay with her and encourage her to do exactly that until she does (assuming you've already taught her this skill, of course!). Avoid sending mixed messages—say, by stopping to search something on Google in the middle of your training and forgetting that you've asked your dog to come to you. You've got to see the training session through to the end.

Also, the more your dog engages in an unwanted behavior, the more ingrained that behavior becomes. So, if your dog is left to bark outside for ten minutes at a time before you intervene, then this barking will likely get worse over time. You want your dog listening to you as close to 100 percent of the time as possible, which means you've got to send her the correct messages as close to 100 percent of the time as possible. What's more, difficulties can be compounded if you have children or other family members who aren't as fully committed to training as you are. It does you no good if you're a stickler at putting a stop to begging at the table but your kid is drop--ping scraps on the floor during dinner. You've all got to be on the same page.

10. KEEP YOUR EXPECTATIONS REALISTIC

It takes a while for a dog to acquire the life experience and guidance from you necessary to know how to behave in a variety of circumstances. You need to dedicate a lot of time to achieve the results you want. By rushing training, you only get mediocre results and wind up delaying true progress in the long run. Just as you wouldn't insist that a preschooler learn to read by reading Shakespeare, you shouldn't insist that your dog behave perfectly after only a few lessons.

You might have encountered other dog trainers who promise that they *can* teach you how to perfectly train a dog in a week or a month or six weeks. However, in my experience, you can't realistically train your dog to behave the way you want in all sorts of situations in such a short amount of time. For example, when I teach people how to teach their dogs, I explain that it will take up to one year to do so. Sure, you can certainly teach the fundamentals such as "sit," "stay," and "come" in a month or two, but it takes a lot more time for your dog to truly understand how to behave in a variety of contexts.

In other words, no matter how well your dog demonstrates that she understands a new principle, remember that it takes time for dogs to internalize that skill and behave as you wish *in unfamiliar places and settings.* Your dog may know "stay" when in a rehearsed training exercise, but how well does she stay when a cat surprises her on a walk or a guest suddenly arrives at your house? To get her staying in those situations, you will frequently need to set up surprise primary training sessions that mimic these real-life situations. You'll also need to snap into training mode whenever the unexpected happens, as I discussed earlier in this chapter.

Sadly, many people have unrealistic expectations, and they expect a dog to, say, stop barking at a person walking in front of the house or to stop pulling on a leash in just a few training sessions. When the dogs don't, these people resort to quick fixes such as choke, prong, or electric collars.

I don't blame everyday people for this. Sadly, the dog training community is largely broken and dysfunctional because there's a massive amount of misinformation out there when it comes to advising the public how to teach dogs. People are left to believe that a dog can be trained in thirty days. And if their progress isn't coming along at this rapid rate, then they assume their dog must require a more disciplined approach. Resorting to these harsh, primitive forms of "communication" only conveys intolerance and a lack of patience and empathy to your dog.

Plus, they don't really work. Too often *learned helplessness*—which is a behavior first identified in dogs by psychologists Martin Seligman and Stephen Maier at the University of Pennsylvania in 1967—is interpreted as training success.[5] But it's not. "Learned helplessness occurs when an animal cannot escape from an aversive situation, and it can no longer effectively fight back to alleviate a punishing circumstance," says John Ciribassi, DVM, DACVB, past president of the American Veterinary Society of Animal Behavior and coeditor of the book *Decoding Your Dog*. "Animals are not learning at these times. Instead, they emotionally close down. Placing any animal in this type of situation is inhumane—I compare it to a person in an abusive situation who has no options to escape the abuse."[6]

Also, keep in mind that there are going to be times when you become frustrated. Occasionally, your dog might take a big step backward in her training. This is all normal. However, you'll need to remain as patient as possible. Progress is unlikely to occur when you are frustrated, so it's okay to take lots and lots of breaks when teaching your dog.

It's the same with kids: patience is critical. Picture a kid who plays baseball. Throughout his years of playing the sport, he'll probably have lots of different coaches. Some he'll love; others not so much. Almost certainly, the ones he'll love are the ones who genuinely and patiently motivate him to do well. They take the time to correct his swing. Instead of yelling at him when he drops a fly ball, they just encourage him to work harder at catching the next one. They routinely practice *with* the kids to show them how to work through difficulties and enthusiastically acknowledge when they are on the right track. I promise you that kids are more likely to excel when they have leadership like this rather than a coach who yells and screams. It's not that the harsher, impatient coaches are completely ineffective, but they likely won't be a contributing factor to furthering a kid's passion for baseball.

In other words, always keep the big picture in mind. Remember, success is usually very slow to come at first. However, if you allow your dog time to grasp new concepts, stay supportive, and follow the advice I've given throughout this chapter, you'll find that she'll learn to love working with you. And that's when you'll really start seeing true progress.

CHAPTER 2

WHY DOGS BEHAVE "BADLY"

I know that many of you picked up this book so you can resolve or prevent your dog's unwanted behaviors, like nipping, lunging on the leash, or not listening in general. Dogs are certainly easy to love, but they very often come with less than desirable instincts and habits that can be difficult to deal with if you don't understand them. This chapter focuses on why dogs sometimes behave less than optimally.

You may be thinking to yourself, "I don't care *why* my dog is chewing up my furniture. I just want him to stop!" And that's totally understandable! However, as you'll learn in this chapter, understanding why dogs likely behave the way that they do is paramount to resolving problems. When the "why" is clearer, so are the solutions.

In other words, you've probably heard the expression, "Treat the cause, not the symptom." Well, this couldn't be truer when it comes to dog training. Actually, this is what inside-out training is all about.

For example, if you figure out that your dog's incessant barking, chewing, or digging stems from not getting enough exercise, then he's probably going to continue those annoying habits until you dedicate more time to engaging him in lots of activities. Or say your dog had a rough start to life and seems to have had negative experiences with men. Well, he might growl or even snap at men until you carefully and deliberately socialize him with them and desensitize him to males.

It's not that different than it is for humans. If you take some pain medication to stop the cramping you have in your foot, then the discomfort is likely to go away. However, if the cause of the foot pain is that you're wearing shoes that are too tight, then you'll continue having pain until you buy a new pair of shoes.

This chapter walks you through the fundamental reasons why your dog might not act as you want him to—so you can refer to it any time you have an issue with your pet. Every subsequent issue addressed in this book also comes with a specific explanation for that particular behavior (like resource guarding or digging). Of course, I also explain what to do about the undesirable behavior.

THE THREE BIGGEST MYTHS REGARDING DOG MISBEHAVIOR

Understanding what *doesn't* cause dogs to misbehave is as important as understanding what does. It's critical not to build training strategies on flat-out myths, but instead to understand the true reasons your dog is behaving a certain way. So, we'll start with the three biggest myths when it comes to dog misbehavior. Then we'll delve into the six proven culprits.

Myth #1: Dogs Are Spiteful

Some people think that when their dog misbehaves it's because he's intentionally trying to displease them or somehow challenge their authority. I know that many of you reading this will say something like, "My dog knows that he's misbehaving but does it anyway." After all, he might put those ears back and turn on those sorry eyes when you discover a chewed-up book or shoe. It's as though he knows he did something wrong.

However, that's not the case. Researchers have found that dogs might look ashamed not because they know they've done something wrong but because they're being scolded.

Ljerka Ostojić, PhD, is a comparative psychologist at Cambridge University in England and lead author of a study in the journal *Behavioural Processes*.[1] She said, "I had a client who had three dogs, and whenever something happened like a shoe was chewed, it was always one [dog in particular] that had the guilty look. Yet often she was not the dog who had done it. She was just the most apprehensive dog, and she got frightened more quickly by her owner's reaction."[2]

Alexandra Horowitz is a scientist who teaches canine cognition, heads the Horowitz Dog Cognition Lab at Barnard College, and is the author of *Inside of a Dog: What Dogs See, Smell, and Know*. She had similar findings in another study.[3] Dogs who were scolded for eating a forbidden treat looked just as guilty regardless of if they had actually obeyed or not. In fact, the dogs most likely to show such behaviors as avoiding eye contact, slinking away, or dropping their heads were those who were innocent but still reprimanded.

So, while dogs are extremely smart, they are far from the calculating, vengeful, plotting creatures that many people shape them up to be. Don't get me wrong—I know it can feel that way sometimes! If you're potty training a dog and you take him for a long walk, but then he comes back in the house and sneaks off to do his business in another room, it might seem like he is trying to break the rules and do things on his terms. You did your part by letting him outside, and he still peed in the house! But in this example, we too often assume that a dog should perform an action— going to the bathroom outside—simply because it should be immediately obvious to him that this makes sense. Also, we assume that it should be equally obvious to him that going inside is not acceptable. This is a mistake though. How should a dog know that he's supposed to hold it until you get around to letting him out? Even then, how's he supposed to make the leap that the grass outside is where he is to do his business?

Remember, dogs are new to our world. There is nothing intuitive to dogs about the nuanced aspects of our culture and expectations. Is it really reasonable, for example, to expect a dog who's only just been introduced to training to differentiate between his plush toy and your fuzzy slippers? How could he possibly know that he can play with the toy but not the slippers unless you've spent a lot of time teaching him just that. Since most of us are anxious to get our dog's training off to a good start, we take steps that are too big and too unrealistic. We then interpret the lack of results to mean that the dog is being vindictive or stubborn.

Planning events in the future, being in firm control of our surroundings and family, and "proving a point" are natural *human* behaviors, but not so much for dogs. Dogs' flagship quality is that they are great at appreciating and living in the present. They aren't premeditated, and they're certainly not spiteful, conniving creatures. They just don't seem to be capable of such emotions. Sure, they may be a little too carefree, loopy, or distractible at times. But they just need the right guidance from you!

Myth #2: Dogs Misbehave Because They Are Trying to Be Dominant

Dominance as an explanation for a dog's behavioral issues is a long-held, though false, belief that unfortunately influences modern dog training culture like no other (though luckily that's changing!). For one thing, there is no agreed upon definition of the term at all. Dominance means different things to different people, and this ambiguity isn't helpful.

Here's what we do know though: we used to think that the wolves the modern dog descended from had a dictatorial "alpha" at the top of each wolf pack who led by significant force and fought for his top status. Much of the dog training community hastily accepted this theory. In fact, leading wolf expert L. David Mech even wrote an acclaimed 1970 book on the subject. However, this older hypothesis was based on an artificial situation: the wolves in the studies were in forced confinement and had no choice but to fight for resources. Wolves in the wild—the wolves our dogs descended from—did not act this way at all. Instead, they behaved more like humans—the "leaders" of the packs, so to speak, were merely parents of offspring. In fact, the packs are very similar to human family structures.[4]

Here's the kicker though: Mech himself eventually refuted the alpha wolf concept. He even asked his publisher to stop printing his book.[5] I tip my hat to him for admitting that he was wrong.

Bottom line: There is absolutely no evidence that dogs inherited a primal desire to move in, take over, and make you subservient to them. (Sadly, many people in the dog training community still build their methods on this unsupported hypothesis, and they use it as a license to train dogs by using force.)

What's more, let's also remember that dogs are not even wolves at all. Humans have aggressively and selectively bred dogs for thousands of years so that they're good at learning and taking direction from people. For instance, we bred dogs who excel at retrieving, assisting with hunting, keeping livestock in line, and even companionship. The modern dog has very little in common with ancient wolves in this regard. And these traits, this proven genetic history of working with and existing well with humans, are what we should always remember when we teach dogs. Understanding this point makes it much easier to accept that teaching a dog is a very natural process.

So, when your dog jumps on you, he's most likely excited to see you and not trying to ignite a revolt. If he passes through a door before you, he's just eager to get outside, not trying to make you submit to him. And if he lies next to you on the couch or in bed? That doesn't mean he thinks he's equal or above you in the family hierarchy. He probably just wants to be close to you.

Myth #3: A Dog's Breed Is to Blame

It's very easy to fall into the trap of attributing your dog's unwanted behaviors to his breed. I always hear comments like, "Huskies won't come when called," "Chihuahuas are yappy and prissy," "Pit Bulls are violent," and "Herding dogs nip at your ankles because they're herding you." Please don't buy into these stereotypes. It's not fair to your dog, and it can really harm your training.

People tend to place entirely too much emphasis on breed and what a dog was bred to do. In other words, too often we think a dog's breed is the primary factor we should take into account when teaching a dog and trying to determine why he's behaving a certain way. The problem with this is that only some dogs of a particular breed seem to adhere to their breed stereotype. However, even when dogs *do* adhere to their breed, their breed is still probably one of the least important factors in that dog's personality. As I explained on page 9, chapter 1, knowing and managing your dog's energy level is the best way to understand him.

Of course, humans did select dogs who were good at specific tasks. In fact, there are countless breeds that we created thousands of years ago to help with tasks such as herding livestock and hunting. However, if you were to take a group of those dogs of the same breed, you'd almost certainly discover that the way they interact with you, each other, and the world varies. These differences are usually significant enough to influence the approach you should take when teaching them or breaking bad habits.

The fact is that dogs of every breed jump up on guests, nip, chase things, destroy property, and don't come when called—and they do these things for very different reasons. While we are right to attempt to understand and make sense of why a dog behaves a certain way, remember that his breed plays only a very small role in this.

Think about it: making a judgment call based on a dog's breed is like predicting people's personalities based on what countries they're from. Just as it's not fair to do so to a human, it's also not fair to make such presumptions about a dog. So please don't.

THE TOP SIX REASONS YOUR DOG MIGHT MISBEHAVE

While we may not assume for certain what our dogs are thinking at any given moment, we can make informed guesses as to what may trigger the behaviors that drive you crazy. That, and the fact that no one knows your dog like you do, will help you get to the bottom of these issues! Like I discussed earlier in this chapter, understanding the likely motivations behind your dog's behavior is the best place to start. So, here are the six biggest culprits.

1. Insufficient Exercise

Want to know the biggest life hack in dog training? It's that exercise resolves most problems. See, it turns out that most of the reactive, misbehaving, out-of-control dogs are the ones who don't have enough of an outlet for their energy. Remember, 90 percent of unwanted behaviors are due to a lack of exercise and the fact that a dog is simply bored! That's 90 percent!

Most annoying habits, anxieties, or hyperactivity can be mitigated greatly with the right kind of exercise. As I explained on page 11, chapter 1, if your dog has an abundance of energy, exercising him early in the day with structured activities like fetch that involve working with a person should satisfy him for a good portion of the day. Regular exercise can even help lower-energy dogs, too, especially regarding issues relating to anxiety and fear.

Also, in the earlier stages of training, it's not even reasonable to expect many unexercised dogs to comply with your requests—especially those mid- to high-energy dogs. Only when your dog has released that energy can he calm down enough to focus on you for the training session.

I know that many dogs are not active, and exercise for those dogs for the purposes of making them more trainable may not be as necessary. However, for those super-energetic dogs, it absolutely is.

It can take many weeks or months to teach a dog how to reliably play fetch, but doing so can make such a massive difference throughout his life. It is really worth the effort. Throughout this book, I'll show you when to strategically use exercise to make training easier. For now, understand that if you'd describe your dog as "wild" or "disobedient," you likely need to prioritize significant exercise.

2. Genetics

Clearly, genetics plays a part in governing how a dog behaves. In fact, a dog's behavior is based on the culmination of his experiences and his genetics. Think about the countless possible combinations you can have of those two things!

I understand that this may be a little confusing as I just told you that you should treat each dog as an individual and not rely on his breed so much to explain his behavior. However, when I'm talking about genetics,

I don't mean breed. I'm talking about traits passed down from generation to generation. Let's take an obvious example. Say two energetic Labradors produce offspring. There is a good chance that at least some of those offspring will also be energetic. However, if two lower-energy Labradors produce offspring, then it's more likely that they'll produce lower-energy puppies. Same exact breed, different genes.

Take a look at dogs who come from puppy mills (the ones sold in the vast majority of pet stores). In a review of various studies published in the *Journal of Veterinary Behavior*, researchers found that dogs sold in pet stores or via the internet are much more likely to experience fear, aggression, separation anxiety, and many other behavioral issues than dogs sold through noncommercial breeders and other sources.[6] Genetics (along with the inhumane way these puppies are often treated, of course) is a major factor in such issues.

In fact, the American Society for the Prevention of Cruelty to Animals explains, "Cruel breeders want to produce as many puppies as possible as quickly as possible. Unlike responsible breeders, they don't screen for inheritable disorders and remove dogs from their breeding program who are less likely to produce healthy puppies."[7]

In other words, responsible breeders make sure that they don't breed dogs who have genetic physical health defects like hip dysplasia and cataracts—and they do the same with behavioral traits such as anxiety, obsessive-compulsiveness, and aggressive behaviors. Puppy mill workers do not. They are focused solely on profit, and they breed dogs with little to no regard for genetic quality.

Also, a study in *BMC Genomics* found that dogs can be genetically predisposed to fear and aggression.[8] Plus, they are genetically programmed to fear either familiar dogs and humans or unfamiliar dogs and humans. Researchers pinpointed twelve genes associated with these behaviors.

Of course, it's difficult to determine if your dog is acting a specific way due to his genetics. That's why I always recommend that when people are looking for dogs, they should meet any potential dog's parents if possible. If not, then at least ask the person who knows the dog you're considering best; find out as much information from that person as you can. For instance, if a dog is from a breeder or if he was born in a shelter, then you should be able to find out quite a bit about at least one, if not both, of his parents *before* you bring him home. I know this isn't always possible, but if it is, then definitely learn what you can.

Again, remember that genetics is only part of the picture. "While genes play a role in canine behavior, it's important to keep in mind that dogs live in a context—the social and physical environments in which they function and develop," explains Karen L. Overall, VMD, PhD, a leading veterinary behaviorist, senior research scientist of biology at the University of Pennsylvania, and founding researcher of the Canine Behavioral Genetics Project. "So while genes tell you what *can* happen, they can't tell you what *will* happen."[9]

3. Change in the Environment

The single fastest way to cause a dog to act uncharacteristically is to change his environment. This is one of those things that you don't account for if you're new to dogs. Environment matters!

As people, we notice a change in the environment ourselves. Think about how you feel when going from a quiet car into a crowded sports stadium or concert, for example. Or how you feel when first entering a party where you don't know a lot of people. The difference is that we've had many years to adjust to and manage such situations. However, don't forget that when you were a toddler, you might have had a meltdown when first experiencing a new place like preschool or even a movie theater. In this respect, dogs are like toddlers.

We often forget how challenging it can be to focus on new things while in new places, and we're people! In your dog's case, there's a reasonable chance that a routine walk can become a "once in a lifetime" experience when he sees a squirrel or a deer for the first time! Imagine what might be going through his mind. He's probably thinking, "There's something new that moves fast and looks fun to chase! I want to see it!" And there goes everything he's learned about walking properly on a leash.

You'll no doubt understand this if you've taught your dog a skill like "sit" in the comfort of your home and then asked him to do the same thing while approaching a dog park or pet supply store. Very often the smells, sights, and sounds of the world prove to be so stimulating that listening to boring things like "sit" and "stay" hardly register. I mean, imagine if an elephant appeared in your neighborhood and someone asked you to calm down and stay put. You probably wouldn't listen to that request as there would be something much more interesting to contend with. So, you might see how getting your dog to stay while so distracted can prove futile if you haven't previously prepared your dog for how to behave in various scenarios.

Plain and simple, dogs don't generalize their skills well in a new place. It takes lots of practice over many months to teach a dog how to listen to you in various environments. Do not hold your dog to the same standards in such places as you do at home unless you've trained him in those places many, many times.

So if your dog gets insanely excited when you take him to the park, for instance, then you should find that increasing the frequency that you go there can help desensitize your dog to all of the fantastic things at the park (like the grass, falling leaves, and even other dogs!). Those frequent visits should help reduce this excitable behavior and normalize the park over time. If your dog went to the park several times a week for a few months, he'd almost certainly start listening to you there.

Throughout this book, I provide you with plenty of options for how to get your dog to listen to you more reliably, and I bring attention to how environment may be impacting your dog's behavior. Also, see chapter 20 for guidance on how to teach your dog to listen in any new environment.

4. Medical Issues

Sometimes a dog's behavioral issue seems to appear suddenly and out of nowhere when there's been no major change to your dog's life or environment. For example, if your dog starts consistently peeing inside the house and you haven't recently moved, then he might have a UTI or other medical issue. Sometimes a dog may growl, nip, or snap at a person or animal uncharacteristically. He might seem extra-anxious. He could suddenly become totally lethargic. These could be signs that a dog is in some type of pain: he might have a stomachache or dental issue or something more serious such as thyroid disease or other illness.

We can all relate to this. Sometimes we don't feel well and are less likely to be in a pleasant mood. We might become grumpy, exhausted, and antisocial. Dogs are no different in this respect. Nobody knows your dog like you do, and you'll likely be the first to realize that something's off with him. Of course, the best way to determine if a medical issue is causing your dog to behave in a way that's not typical is to visit your vet to get to the bottom of it.

5. Lack of Socialization

A lack of socialization at a young age seems to be a major cause of behavioral issues in dogs. In fact, the American Veterinary Medical Association says that the socialization period—which occurs primarily between six and fourteen weeks—is the time of life for a puppy when "providing diverse, positive experiences can prevent the development of fearful responses and subsequent behavioral problems."[10]

Why is this the case? Like humans, dogs are impressionable. Certain events and experiences can contribute to how a dog is likely to react to those things in the future. For example, if a puppy experiences a kid pulling his tail, the puppy may continue to assume smaller humans with higher-pitched voices are likely to cause harm or annoyance.

Also, if a puppy is simply not exposed to something frequently enough, then he may become overexcited, fearful, or even aggressive when he later encounters that thing. As another example, it seems that a lot of dogs are fearful of men. It could be that a dog had a negative experience with a man when he was a puppy. Or he might not have been exposed to men enough when he was younger.

See, ideally, if you have a puppy, it's critical you go out of your way to provide him with an array of experiences. Expose him to dogs, cats, and other animals. (Of course, check with your vet first to make sure your puppy is sufficiently vaccinated for such encounters—but note that experts often say your dog doesn't have to be *fully* vaccinated for such exposure.[11])

Let your dog play with children and get petted by strangers of any gender and of all races and sizes. Turn on your hair dryer, expose your dog to someone with a beard or glasses, let him see a motorcycle race by, and make sure he hears the garbage truck on your street.

You get it—the more experiences, the better. When you take a pro-active approach to exposing your dog to lots of new things and making sure to provide fun, enjoyable outcomes surrounding those things—like treats, playtime, or some affection—then dogs are less likely to have social issues. Also, even though six to fourteen weeks is the critical socialization period, keep making it a point to expose your puppy to new experiences throughout his first eight to twelve months. Every little bit of socialization helps.

I know not everyone gets a puppy. Many of you have saved a homeless dog from your local shelter or adopted an adult dog from a rescue group. Maybe your dog appears to be uncomfortable around men, children, big dogs, beach balls, or something else. What are you to do now that these perceptions are ingrained within your dog? The good news is hope is far from lost.

While it may take some additional time and patience, you can likely overcome these issues with basic counterconditioning, the process of creating a pleasant association with something that currently causes a dog to act unpleasantly. For example, if your dog is scared of men, then repeated exposure to nice men who play with your dog and give him treats may elicit a different reaction from him over time. Or if your dog currently goes bananas when the vacuum is turned on, then gradually turning on the vacuum for short periods of time while rewarding him with good treats may ultimately help him act much more calmly next time you're doing some housecleaning.

This, combined with exercise, continued socialization, and controlling your dog's environment, is likely to yield great results. For example, if your dog is wary of children and he is around a child, make sure that the child and your dog do not interact to prevent escalating your dog's uneasiness. Then, you could take steps to help your dog become more comfortable around kids by arranging mellow encounters where, say, a child sits nearby while you play with your dog and possibly moves closer over time. This is desensitization at work!

With some patience and understanding and making sure your pet knows he can trust you, most dogs show dramatic improvement on issues relating to socialization over time. However, there isn't always a fix for dogs with more extreme social issues. Some dogs should never be around cats, for example, while others may never like certain surfaces (like grass or slippery floors), loud noises, or particular environments. And that's okay!

We must accept our dogs for who they are. Yet, rest assured that if you follow the principles outlined throughout the book, you are likely to see improvement for most issues.

6. A Lapse in Training

Never blame your dog! It's easy to hold dogs to a high standard because they usually demonstrate how smart they really are at a very young age. So we assume that if they're not conforming to our expectations, then it must be their fault. However, if your dog chews something up, has an accident in the house, or consistently jumps all over houseguests, then you must understand that that's a reflection of how well you have taught your dog the fundamentals.

Whenever there is a breakdown in how you want your dog to behave, ask yourself if you're controlling the environment well enough, exercising your dog, and doing everything I addressed throughout chapter 1. Also, keep in mind that learning doesn't happen by insisting or getting mad or frustrated. Instead, learning occurs when you break things down to where they're easy enough for your dog to understand, and then you acknowledge every small success. Sometimes you have to take two steps backward and one step forward to see results. The great thing is that, when you remain patient and you and your dog start to click, you really start to see incredible progress!

CHAPTER 3

THE CRITICAL SKILLS

Before we delve into the behavioral issues and how to handle each one, it's important to make sure you have a good handle on the fundamental skills every dog should know. A lot of these skills are actually the key to resolving many unwanted behaviors.

In my first book, *Zak George's Dog Training Revolution: The Complete Guide to Raising the Perfect Pet with Love,* I cover these skills in great depth. And, of course, I address them on my YouTube channel.

In this chapter, I want to give you a quick refresher. Here are the essential skills your dog needs to know before you can address all the common training problems I cover in this book.

SIT AND DOWN

I often teach these two skills together because they rely on the same concept: lure training. *Lure training* is using a treat to coax your dog into a certain physical position. Here's how to teach these skills:

Sit

1. Hold a small treat between your thumb and forefinger and make sure your dog sees it. Keeping it very close to your dog's nose, move it over the bridge of her nose and up so that she lifts her nose directly up toward the ceiling or sky. This is lure training at its best! Just make sure you keep the treat and your dog's nose close at all times, almost like magnets.

2. As your dog's head tilts farther back, usually she will automatically sit down. (If she jumps up, you are likely starting with the treat too high above her face.) The second your dog's hind legs touch the ground, say, "Yes! Sit!" once, and then give her the treat. Repeat this drill often.

3. Once your dog gets the hang of this, you can turn the lure into whatever hand signals you'd like to use. For example, you might say, "Sit!" as you point to the floor with your finger.

Down

1. Ask your dog to sit and then hold a treat very close to her nose. Very slowly move the treat down to the ground or down and inward toward her chest so that your dog follows the lure into a down position. When she lies down, say something like, "Great! Down!" and give her the treat.

2. You also have the option of "capturing" a down. For example, if you notice your dog is about to lie down—say, she's turning in a circle or goes over to her bed—this would be your cue to say, "Down" as your dog performs the action. Over time, your dog will start making the connection between her behavior and the word *down*.

LEAVE IT

This skill is a fundamental part of all distraction training. It can also save your dog's life—especially if she's the type to eat any bit of litter or other objects she finds on the ground. Here's how to teach this skill:

1. Put a piece of food in your hand and make sure your dog knows that it's there. You might need to close your hand at first, especially if your dog is frantically trying to get at the food.

2. Within a minute or two, most dogs either become distracted by something else or lose interest for a microsecond. That's when you immediately say, "Yes, leave it!" and then give your dog the food. Repeat this step a few times.

3. Next, place a piece of food on the floor in front of her. Again, your dog will probably lunge for it, so put your hand over the food, restricting her access to it, and say, "No." Saying "no" always has a consequence; in this case it's that she can't have the food.

4. Begin to slowly reveal the food to your dog, making sure you cover it up each time your dog tries to get it prematurely. When your dog doesn't go for it even for a fraction of a second, enthusiastically say, "Yes, leave it!" Then, pick up the reward and give it to her so she learns that rewards always come directly from you. Repeat this often.

5. As your dog shows that she understands "leave it," begin doing surprise primary "leave it" training sessions to start simulating real-life distractions. For instance, if you're cooking in the kitchen, drop a morsel of food on the ground and ask your dog to "leave it." Practice this as much as you can.

LOOK AT ME/WATCH ME

"Look at me" (or its variant "watch me") is also one of the most important skills your dog needs to learn. First, if your dog doesn't have eye contact with you, then it's that much more difficult to teach her. Also, having your dog look at you is a critical step in making sure she listens to you around distractions. Here's how to teach this skill:

1. Get at eye level with your dog and hold a treat directly in front of your eyes. Your dog will probably look at the treat and, as soon as you have eye contact with her, say, "Yes, look at me!" Start very close, keeping your training bubble—the distance between your dog's eyes and your own—very small. Repeat this a few times.

2. Next, point to your eyes but without a treat in your hand. That way your dog is now looking at your finger, not at the food. Again, as soon as she looks at you, say, "Yes, look at me!" and then you can give her a treat with your other hand. Reward generously for weeks on this one.

3. Gradually stretch the training bubble by working your way up to being able to stand up. The goal is to be able to stand up and hold your dog's gaze for up to ten seconds as she remains in front of you. Once you have your dog's eyes on you, you'll know you have her attention!

LEAVE IT/LOOK AT ME COMBO

Now that you've learned "leave it" and "look at me," it's time to combine them. *This is a magical exercise* because together these skills are the key to getting your dog to listen to you in the face of distractions. Your dog might leave something alone during a chill training session at home, but it's very different asking her to do the same while you're on a walk and she encounters a squirrel running by, another dog, or litter on the sidewalk. The purpose of the "leave it/look at me" drill is to make sure your dog understands the concept of choosing to look at you *even when she sees something she wants.* Here's how to teach this skill:

1. In your home, put your dog on leash and do a basic "leave it" drill with a piece of meat. However, this time when your dog leaves the meat alone, encourage her to look at you by saying, "Look at me." When she does, say, "Yes" and reward her. By doing this, you're getting your dog's attention on you instead of on a real piece of meat right in front of her!

2. Change things up a little bit. Take a favorite toy, drop it in front of your dog, and have her repeat the "leave it/look at me" drill. Practice this in a variety of ways as much as possible.

3. Now start walking around your house with your dog. As you do so, throw the meat or toy away, toward, or to the left or right of her, asking her to "leave it/look at me" each time. The idea is that you are preparing your dog for real-life distractions by showing her how to respond to mild distractions at first.

4. If you are doing well with this, move the lesson to your front yard or driveway. Since you're changing a variable in your training—the location—your dog might be thrown off at first. Slow down and be patient while she gets the hang of it. As your dog gets better at this drill, take the opportunity to practice it in various situations.

COME

This is another vital skill that all dogs need to learn. The last thing you want is your dog running into harm's way only to ignore you when you call her back to you. Here's how to teach this skill:

1. Starting in a quiet, familiar environment, have your dog between you and, if possible, another person. If you're teaching "come" by yourself, keep your dog on a long lead leash. Start with your dog a few feet from you. Show her that you have a treat in hand, and then call her to you in a really happy, enthusiastic voice. When she takes even one step toward you, praise her and say, "Great! Come!" Give her the reward. The key here is to make your dog realize that by coming to you, really awesome things are going to happen for her. If you're working with another person, have him or her repeat the same drill so that your dog is running back and forth between the two of you.

2. Gradually increase the distance at which you ask your dog to come. If at any time during training, your dog stops coming to you, decrease the distance and slowly try to work back to that point. Also, practice this randomly and often when your dog doesn't expect it, such as while you're watching TV or sitting at a kitchen table working. This is how you'll begin to help her generalize the concept outside of the initial training sessions.

3. Once you've succeeded repeatedly at home, it's time to take your training sessions outside. Over the next several months of training, take your dog to lots of different places to practice "come." This is how you'll teach your dog to generalize this skill in various environments. Just make sure those areas are fenced in; otherwise, have your dog on a long lead leash so that you ultimately always have complete control.

STAY

You can divide "stay" training into three categories: stay for a period of time, stay with distance, and most important, stay while distracted. The key is adding only one new variable at a time so you don't confuse your dog. Here's how to teach these skills:

Stay for a Period of Time

1. Remaining close to your dog, ask her to sit and reward her when she does. As soon as she sits, put your palm facing her as though you're telling her to stop. Find the tiniest reason to acknowledge a stay at this point. So if she doesn't move, even for a split second, say, "Great, stay!" and reward her. If she does move, calmly say, "No" and try again.

2. Once you've mastered a brief stay for a few seconds, gradually add time to it. Start with one second, then two, and so on, working up to thirty seconds. Mix up the time periods you ask for along the way to avoid being too predictable. When you're ready to release your dog from a stay, say something like, "Okay" or whatever word or phrase you choose to let your dog know the stay is over. If your dog breaks her stay at any point, say, "No," withhold the reward, and try the drill again for a shorter period of time.

Stay with Distance

1. Starting just a few inches from your dog, ask for a basic stay. If you are on the ground and your dog is particularly clingy, begin by moving just your head a few inches away. If your dog holds her stay, reward her for the minor progress. Work up to being able to stand up as she holds her stay. Reward her.

2. Now add distance. Take a tiny step backward and then return promptly to your dog and reward her before she has a chance to move. Notice that you're *not pausing* at the end of her stay yet. Most people intuitively do this, and it can delay your progress. Remember to *change one variable at a time*. In this case, the variable is "moving away," not "moving away and also pausing."

3. Move backward one step, then two, and then three. Slowly work your way up to greater distances. Once you've reached your desired distance, always immediately return to your dog and reward her before she breaks out of the stay. If your dog fails two times in a row, you are asking too much of her too soon, so decrease the distance the next two or three times. Don't rush this process! For some dogs, you may need a few training sessions to work up to three feet; others may achieve forty feet during the first training session.

4. Once your dog is staying at a given distance twenty to thirty times in a row, work on adding more time at various distances. In other words, now you can begin pausing. This is a really special moment, because you are now combining duration and distance in a single exercise. At first, be content with a one- or two-second stay with some distance. Work your way up to thirty seconds over the next week or so.

Stay While Distracted

1. Teaching your dog to stay at doorways is a great way to introduce this concept because you can work in a familiar environment (your home) with a more distracting environment at a near distance (the outside). Of course, safety first: Practice this in a fenced-in yard or on leash if there's a street in front of your door. Also, practice this at a time when you're not actually opening the door in real life—say, to let in a guest—so you're not distracted either. To start, ask your dog to sit by the door and then stay. Since an open door is a fairly significant distraction by itself, start small. Most dogs know that when your hand goes near the doorknob, something exciting is about to happen. So, touch the doorknob. If your dog doesn't budge, reward her before she even has a chance to break her stay. Repeat this several times.

2. Now take a more significant, but still fairly easy step: open the door an inch or two and then close it. Again, if your dog holds her stay, give her a treat and authentic praise! Gradually open the door farther until it's wide open. Have your dog stay for a few

seconds and encourage her to look at you. After doing this several times, notice that your dog automatically begins to anticipate that you want her to look at you and does so. Give her an extra-big reward for such an accomplishment.

3. If at any point your dog breaks her stay, simply say, "No" and shut the door. Limiting access to the place your dog wants to go—in this case, outside—is the consequence for breaking the stay. You should also withhold the reward.

4. If all is going well, ask your dog to stay and make the outside really exciting. Throw a fun toy or even a treat out the door. If your dog resists the urge to run outside, celebrate with her! You may have to cut back on the length of the stay since you've added a new variable here, but you can eventually work up to longer periods of time. Reward for the smallest increments of success here.

5. For the next year, I strongly recommend insisting that your dog hold a sit and a stay for five to ten seconds at every open door leading outside before allowing her to walk through it. Be really consistent. This is so important!

PART II

THE ISSUES

CHAPTER 4

BARKING

A couple of years ago I was in a restaurant in New Orleans when a woman named Catherine, a fan of my YouTube series, came up to say, "Hi!" I asked her about her dog and how training was going. She told me that things were going very well . . . except for the barking. Catherine explained that her dog, Arwen, a small mixed-breed dog, barked like crazy every time someone came to the door. She said it was almost impossible to get Arwen under control. I happened to have been looking for a dog with this exact issue, so I asked Catherine if I could film a lesson with her dog. Catherine quickly agreed.

Arwen was a handful and certainly lived up to her reputation. While she was generally vocal, I decided to focus the lesson on getting her quiet when there was knocking at the door. She gave me a run for my money, but ultimately had an outstanding first lesson. The video, which is on my YouTube channel, is called *How to Train Your Dog to Stop Barking*.

Unwanted barking can really get out of control in no time if you don't take the proper steps to discourage it. I'm not talking about an alert bark or two. I'm talking about barking that goes on for minutes . . . or an hour. I'm also talking about barking that seems to occur for no reason. You know, the kind that drives you crazy while you're trying to work, watch

TV, or just enjoy a bit of silence at home. Then, there are other dogs who bark continually as if to demand food or attention. This is known as *demand barking.*

While I show you the steps to mitigate any kind of barking in this chapter, just know that most dogs are *still* likely to bark if something is out of the ordinary. And that's a good thing! Dogs are still dogs, so it's unrealistic to expect dogs to remain completely quiet all the time any more than it is to expect a child to always be silent. However, you can teach your dog that he can alert you with a few barks when there's an urgent or unusual situation, but he should otherwise remain quiet. In other words, you can nip prolonged barking in the bud! This chapter will help you do just that.

WHY DO DOGS BARK?

Dogs bark as a way to communicate. They bark to greet people and when they're excited and want your attention. They also bark when they are concerned or afraid. In fact, a lot of us depend on our dogs to bark, alerting us when someone or something is nearby. Dogs are uniquely qualified to do that—they are particularly aware of their surroundings in ways that we are not. For instance, while humans typically can hear sounds within the frequencies of 20Hz and 20,000 Hz, dogs can hear between 40Hz and 60,000 Hz, depending on their age and health.[1] Plus, dogs' ears have more mobility than human ears, and they are often shaped in a way that helps with hearing.

Unfortunately, our dogs don't know that, well, we don't want to necessarily be alerted to *every single thing* that they detect. This can become a major nuisance for people—especially if your dog has a particularly loud bark like mine does.

Also, keep in mind that most unwanted barking occurs because a dog doesn't have a sufficient mental and physical outlet. Unwanted barking is most common with underexercised and bored dogs. If your dog has pent-up energy, make sure you are exercising him according to his exercise requirements. With those really high-energy dogs, remember that they will likely need regular exercise throughout their lives, and almost certainly just prior to the training exercises I detail in this chapter.

Perhaps the most difficult type of barking to resolve is the kind that's related to a dog's anxiety at being left alone—whether for a few hours or even just thirty seconds (which is the case for a lot of puppies). Have a little sympathy: just like infants, puppies are just learning about the world and they don't intuitively understand why you'd ever leave them alone. You're their person, and they want to be with you! They *will* learn that it's okay to be alone sometimes, but that can take a bit of time. If you have an older dog who is moderately to severely anxious about being left alone, check out chapter 16 to learn how to handle separation anxiety. Remember, to really tackle behavioral issues, we have to address the cause of a problem, not just the symptoms.

WHAT TO DO ABOUT BARKING

As with virtually everything in dog training, the ideal time to address unwanted barking is *not* when your dog is already having a barking fit. For example, if your dog tends to bark excessively when someone comes to the door and you try to teach your dog to stop barking in that moment, you'll likely be unsuccessful. Dogs do not respond well when their teacher's attention is divided. In this example, you might be trying to welcome your guest *and* get your dog quiet at the same time. That's not going to work. Instead, you need to plan primary training sessions to minimize barking. Here's what you can do:

1. A prerequisite to these exercises is that you have taught a basic "sit" and "stay" with minor distractions and a solid "leave it/ look at me" combo. (See chapter 3.) Reliable attention is critical when trying to override your dog's impulse to bark at something. Also, make sure your dog has gotten some exercise before the training session.

2. Next, set up training sessions where your dog might likely bark. For example, maybe your dog barks when he hears a knock at the door. So, you could ask a friend or neighbor to knock at your door for this exercise. First, ask your dog to sit and then stay to make sure you have his committed attention. Use a really good currency here like boiled chicken since you'll be challenging your dog. (In this case, food might be a better reward than playtime since you don't want your dog getting too riled up.)

3. Have the other person knock *just once* lightly. Because you know that the knock is coming, you are in an ideal position to immediately request that your dog keeps his attention on you. Tell him, "Look at me." And when he does, give him a bit of his currency. Since we're talking about just one knock here, this should go smoothly pretty early in your training. If it doesn't and your dog still barks, then take a step back in your training. Have the other person only approach the door without knocking or ask him or her to just stay on the sidewalk outside your house—whatever it takes to achieve even a moment of success.

4. Now let's make things a little bit more challenging. Ask your helper to knock twice this time. Continue doing this until your dog reliably gives you attention as the knocks occur. Work your way up *gradually* to a steady knock that might resemble a real-life knock—say, four or five raps on the door—and ask the person to throw in a "Hello? Anyone home?" in a loud voice. See, that's how training works—nice and slow. No single step should ever be considerably more difficult than the previous one. Repeat this exercise as often as possible, ideally twice a day for two to four weeks.

5. Change up variables creatively as your dog starts to get the hang of the rules. For instance, maybe your dog barks at the vacuum cleaner. Use the same logic: don't wait until it's time to vacuum. Instead, turn on the vacuum for a half second and reward for quiet behavior before your dog has a chance to bark, gradually increasing the time that the vacuum is on to two seconds, ten seconds, one minute, three minutes, and so on. The real key

with these exercises is that you must be in a position to control and manipulate the things that cause your dog to bark.

6. So far, we've put our dog in a position of anticipating the knock in a highly artificial situation that we set up. Now it's time for those surprise primary lessons—ones that seem more spontaneous from your dog's perspective and catch him completely off guard. However, whereas before, both you and your dog knew there was a training session under way, now only you do. You are still in full control of the knocking and prepared to either reinforce good behavior or redirect undesired behavior.

7. When you want to start a surprise primary lesson, grab a treat nonchalantly when your dog is not paying much attention and knock on the door, kitchen counter, or coffee table one or two times. Then instantly request your dog's attention before he even has a chance to bark. Vigorously reward the early achievements. Even if you have to hold the treat directly to your dog's nose and reward for a fraction of a second of silence, then consider this an early success. If your dog continues to struggle with this surprise exercise, then take a step back and master the previous steps more thoroughly.

8. Over the next few weeks, routinely and creatively find ways to catch your dog off guard. Maybe you know that a delivery person is coming to the door. Instead of prematurely opening the door, allow him to knock at the door. When he does, get your dog's attention on you by asking for a "look at me." Reward accordingly. At first, you might experience some setbacks. Remember, we are teaching our dogs to override their very real instincts to bark when something has their attention. This is no small feat. Don't be deterred, stay the course, and most importantly keep things fun and positive for both of you! Like us, dogs have their good days and their not-so-good days. Be prepared to reduce or increase the difficulty as needed during any given training session.

9. So far, I've gone over how to teach your dog not to bark at all. While that's a good way to gain traction on this issue, I strongly recommend that you ultimately remain tolerant of minor barking. For example, one or two barks might be okay when someone knocks at your door or gets close to your property. If so, let those barks go as if to say, "Thank you for letting me know someone is out there." However, if the barking continues after those one or two barks, *then* escort your dog away and apply all of the steps I've gone over in this section. Your dog will learn that it's okay to bark a few times when he wants to alert you to something, but *just* a few times.

GETTING READY FOR THE REAL DEAL

What do you do when your dog's barking really catches *you* off guard? This is where those very important secondary training sessions come into play. Remember, secondary sessions are unplanned training sessions. That's where the magic happens, because they make *you* a better trainer since you'll need to be able to tune into your dog quickly. That's awkward for most people in the beginning, but if you commit to this now, you'll be a pro in no time.

At first, your dog is still likely to bark in spite of your efforts because he's legitimately surprised, and you are likely to be slow at getting this training session under way at first since you're surprised, too. However, if you've thoroughly practiced your surprise primary sessions, success is likely to happen quickly since those planned "surprises" are the same thing as the real deal from your dog's perspective.

The key is that you have to be able to get to your dog's currency fast when you are forced into a secondary training session. Luckily, most dogs let on that they seem to be contemplating barking at something before they actually do it. Maybe they hear a motorcycle driving past the front of your house, and they do a little alert head tilt. You should know from past experience that this simple movement is often followed by barking. The faster you can get at redirecting your dog's attention to you during these subtle moments, the faster you will resolve this type of barking. You'll have to put in some practice to get that timing solid.

The thing about these impromptu training sessions is that you are usually using dog treats stashed by the front door or in the part of the house where your dog tends to bark the most since chicken and other meats don't stay fresh when left out. While treats are enough incentive for a lot of dogs, in some cases, your dog may be so overwhelmed with excitement that, as I mentioned previously, you may need to place the treat *right* at his nose and lure him toward you to get his attention. If this is unsuccessful and your dog is more interested in barking than paying attention to you and receiving a treat, then take a step back and do more of the primary training exercises.

In moments where your dog is barking like crazy and you are unable for one reason or another to teach him in that moment, it might be ideal to at least put him in another room so that there is a consequence for the undesirable behavior. In this instance, that consequence is no access to the exciting thing that's causing him to bark. Your version of this when on a walk might be to walk abruptly away from the thing catching your dog's attention. If necessary and if possible, you could even pick him up to get away from the situation.

PREVENTING BARKING WHEN YOU'RE NOT HOME

If your dog tends to bark excessively when you are out of the house, things are a bit trickier. You'll need to implement the training steps above very often while at home so that your dog comes to accept that quiet is preferred in the house. Thoroughly exercising your dog based on his physical requirements just before leaving home is also likely to significantly reduce long, sustained barking. Think about it: if they're tired after exercise, most dogs will relax when their people are gone.

Of course, putting your dog somewhere in the house where he can't see all the activity going on outside—like away from windows with views of the street in front of your house—can help curtail his barking, too.

In general, the best way to approach barking due to separation anxiety is to get your dog comfortable with being alone for minutes at a time when you *are* at home. Gradually insist on longer periods of acceptable behavior. For example, if your dog is uncomfortable when alone, start a training session right after a long walk or fetch session. Place your dog in another room (without you) and see if he's quiet for a few seconds or minutes.

For those who bark, set a timer on your phone to track how long your dog barks in a room alone before ultimately settling down. This is a great way to measure progress over time. When a dog is barking in another room, it can seem like an eternity. Very often, though, it's only a few minutes. For example, if you notice that it takes seven minutes for your dog to stop barking, take advantage of knowing that and reward him when he is quiet after six minutes. A food or play reward isn't usually necessary here as access to the more desirable environment where you are is usually rewarding in and of itself.

Teaching your dog this kind of conduct requires you to do variations of this exercise over time. For example, if you have guests coming over, exercise your dog just before their arrival and place him in another room for a little bit. You literally want your dog used to being alone when you are still in a position to teach him. Since you've exercised your dog, compliance should come somewhat easily. If your dog is quiet during those first few minutes, let him out to enjoy the company! If he barks, he's not yet ready for this exercise. However, stick with it and you ought to notice a notable reduction of barking over the next few weeks. And when your dog is quieter while you're out of sight but still at home, then he'll be quieter when you're out of the house, too.

HANDLING MULTIPLE DOGS WHO BARK

If you have multiple dogs, you'll need to work on excessive barking with one dog at a time to get it solid. I know that means more work, but trying to teach more than one dog a new skill at a time is likely to be futile. In other words, it's ideal to have only one dog at a time out during primary training sessions. If you find that you are caught off guard and two or more of your dogs spontaneously begin to bark, prioritize the dog with the most training in this area. That way you can at least get one dog quiet so you can then work on training the other one (or ones). In some cases, once you get one dog quiet, the other dog or dogs might follow suit!

CHAPTER 5

CHEWING

Chewing is very common among dogs of all ages. For puppies, they usually chew because they're teething. For older dogs, they might chew due to boredom or anxiety or because chewing has simply become their favorite pastime. However, regardless of the reason, having a puppy or dog who likes to chew can be a major nuisance. First, they can destroy items in your home. Also, they can accidentally ingest something harmful ranging from toilet paper, rocks, books, and stuffed toys to socks, underwear, shoes, and hairbands. I hear of far too many dogs who have to have their stomachs pumped or objects surgically removed. In other words, if your dog likes to chew, it's critical to take steps to protect both her and your belongings.

I filmed a video on this topic with a dog named Winston, a very large rescue dog who had an appetite for recreational chewing. He'd chew just about anything he could find. He was otherwise very well behaved and as sweet as could be—but he'd shred a couch in no time if left to his own devices.

Overall, working with Winston on his obsession with chewing was a smooth process. Why? Because Winston's overall foundation of training made it much easier. See, when training dogs, you can't really deal with each issue on a stand-alone basis. There are fundamentals that must be in place (such as "sit," "leave it," and "look at me") to get results on other issues (see chapter 3 for a refresher). Because Winston's people were so good about basic training, it wasn't that difficult to get Winston to take his attention off of things that were inappropriate to chew and to focus on acceptable things instead.

The YouTube video with Winston, *How to Stop Your Dog from Chewing*, is certainly a great place to start when working on this issue. This chapter also covers everything you need to know.

WHY DO PUPPIES CHEW?

When puppies are teething, their need to chew things is intense for about six months until their adult teeth come in. (Yes, just like babies!) So, during this time, puppies require a variety of different things to chew on that have different textures. At one moment, they may prefer something soft like a plush toy or one of your slippers. Another time, they might crave something harder like a safe, natural bone or a coffee table leg. It's unrealistic to expect teething dogs to understand the difference between what's okay for them to chew and what's not. That's why it's our responsibility to provide a selection of safe chewable items as our puppies teethe and work through this process.

WHY DO ADULT DOGS CHEW?

Incessant chewing doesn't just automatically stop because a dog has all of her adult teeth. Puppy chewing can certainly evolve into recreational chewing, especially if a dog wasn't properly taught not to chew whatever she pleased when she was a puppy.

I see this a lot with shelter dogs. It's common for many dogs to enter the shelter at a young age (many are even born there) and get adopted when they are, say, nine months to a year old. Since most of these dogs haven't experienced regimented and regular training, some of them still chew anything in sight.

Keep in mind that if a dog is new to living inside a house, as many rescue dogs are, the temptation to chew on stuff like your furniture and personal belongings might be very enticing as she's never seen these things before. Remember, patience is key. Dogs just need to learn right from wrong.

Dogs—especially those with a lot of energy—also might chew because they are bored. Try to see it from their perspective: their genetics are telling them to "Go! Go! Go!" so chewing on things is one way that these dogs like to occupy themselves if there's little else to do.

Another possible culprit: Excessive chewing could be a symptom of anxiety. Some dogs are more likely to chew when you leave them alone for a significant period of time (even if adequately exercised) or during thunderstorms or other events.

WHAT TO DO ABOUT CHEWING

First and most importantly, make sure your dog can't chew something that can harm her. That's why it's critical that you pet proof your house as soon as you bring home your new dog, if not sooner. For instance, make sure all electrical cords are out of reach or unplugged, secure your garbage can, and keep baby latches on low cabinets that contain laundry detergent, pesticide, paint, antifreeze, or any other potentially toxic household items. Make sure your laundry basket is secure, too. My YouTube video *Everything You Need to Be Prepared for Your New Puppy* touches upon getting your home safe and ready for your pet. Here's what else to do about chewing:

1. Control your dog's environment. If you do, then she won't be able to sneak off and chew something off limits. Remember, every time you drop your guard and your dog chews something she shouldn't, you're only increasing the odds that the behavior will recur. In other words, to resolve an unwanted behavior,

you need to make great efforts to prevent those behaviors from occurring *at all*. That means attaching your dog's leash to your belt loop or making sure she's in a pet-proofed area at times you can't watch her, like in a crate or playpen or in a gated space such as a laundry room. This goes for young and untrained older dogs alike.

2. Find acceptable, safe things for your dog to chew on. This is especially true for puppies. They *really* need to chew—teething can be painful, and they require that release. Provide your dog with plenty of safe bones, age-appropriate toys, and other items to chew on throughout the day.

3. If you have an older dog who's chewing things she's not supposed to, there's a high probability she's bored and not getting enough exercise and extracurricular training. So, addressing chewing with dogs like this is more about addressing their boredom through general training and exercise than just about teaching them they can't chew whatever they want. Ideal exercise is the kind that involves working with a person! Remember, fetch is one of the best options. See page 149, chapter 17 for a step-by-step description of how to teach it.

4. If you think your dog is chewing because she's, say, fearful or experiencing separation anxiety, then you need to tackle those issues first. Remember, it's critical to always treat the cause, not the symptoms. I address fear issues in chapter 15 and separation anxiety in chapter 16.

5. Once you've taught a basic "leave it" (as I cover on page 47, chapter 3), practice it dozens of times a day with many different objects. For example, pick up a sock, shoe, or any everyday object your dog might be interested in chewing and set it in front of her. Ask her to "leave it," if she attempts to sniff it (which most curious dogs will). Reward her when she does leave it alone. The key is that you want your dog ignoring her temptation to act impulsively and pay attention to you instead. These "leave it" training exercises really enable dogs to broadly understand

how to leave things alone in a variety of contexts. Eventually, you ought to be able to say, "Leave it" when you see your dog about to start chewing something that's off limits, and she will readily comply. Bottom line: Your goal is to teach your dog to leave things alone by default. By practicing with a variety of items, she'll come to generalize the concept to all objects.

6. When you catch your dog red-handed, launch into a secondary training session. For instance, let's say you see your dog chewing on a shoe. While your first instinct is probably to pull her away, refrain from doing so if possible (unless the object is very valuable to you or toxic to her, of course). Instead, first interrupt her, maybe by clapping your hands or calling her name. Next, get her attention on you and quickly substitute the item she was chewing with an acceptable object such as a bone or chew toy. Make sure it's one that your dog really likes! This new bone or chew toy can be the reward itself. If this is unsuccessful, you may want to grab one of your nearby treats to lure her away from the object she was chewing and *then* offer the desirable and acceptable chew toy. You'll need to be a master at redirecting your dog during this interim period. It might take dozens of attempts before your dog begins to make the connection, "Oh! I get it! I can chew *this*, but not *that*."

7. Ignore quick fixes. There are some funny ways that people have attempted to resolve destructive chewing. For example, maybe you've heard that spraying something with a bad tasting spray is a viable way to stop chewing. First, just because something tastes bad doesn't mean it's immune to being chewed up by a dog. Second, this approach is outside-in training. Even in the best case, where your dog doesn't chew the couch because it tastes bad, are you really expected to spray every single object in your house that you think your dog might chew? What happens when the spray wears off or when you are in a new place? That's why when it comes to teaching dogs, always resist shortcuts and favor the more thorough approach instead.

CHAPTER 6

JUMPING UP

Jumping up is one of the most common behavioral issues that I deal with. Some people might not mind this behavior at all, while others would do anything to make it stop. However, many people (like me!) are probably somewhere in the middle—they sometimes enjoy when their dog jumps on them, but not always. The way I see it, you can arrange it so your dog can jump on you if you'd like, but *only* with your permission!

I first want to promise you that dogs can absolutely learn when it's okay to jump and when it's not. Having raised three world-class Frisbee dogs, I can tell you that I relied on my dogs spring-boarding off of my body into the air to catch discs on a daily basis. Did this mean that they'd jump on everyone else or even on me when I didn't ask them to do so? Of course not! In fact, it was customary for me to bring my dogs out at the end of a show to let people pet them. Clearly, allowing a dog to jump on members of the public would not have been ideal. However, my dogs—the same ones who only moments earlier were jumping on my back and then leaping off of it and into the air—sat patiently while their fans adored them.

In other words, I've got you covered. I'll teach you how to allow your dog to jump on *your* terms, whether that means occasionally or not at all.

WHY DO DOGS JUMP?

Few behaviors are more natural to a dog than jumping. When a dog jumps on you, it just means he's excited to see you and eager to interact with you! Also, he has likely been rewarded for this behavior in the past—you or your guests shower him with attention—and you haven't taught him the proper way to greet people. It most certainly does *not* mean that he's trying to dominate you in any way, as some dog trainers claim despite the mountain of information that suggests otherwise.[1] That's just a myth, which I discuss in more detail in chapter 2.

One of the things that makes stopping unwanted jumping challenging is that your dog is genuinely happy to see you or others and doesn't know the proper way to express those feelings yet! See, it's natural for dogs to want to greet us at our faces. Think about it—when dogs greet one another they do so by sniffing each other's faces. Of course, they can't easily do this with humans. Since they are close to the ground, they attempt to close that distance by jumping.[2]

I recently filmed a video on jumping with Zeus, a giant Belgian Shepherd. Zeus is the kind of dog who is overflowing with energy and emotion. He was very happy—and he loved showing it! Zeus's family sought my help to see how they could better get through to this not-so-gentle giant. When I first met him, my immediate thought was, "Wow! We really have to get this dog's jumping under control." When he would jump, he was as tall as me on his hind legs! I knew he could easily knock someone over and cause some harm. Zeus was an extreme case for sure, but he really started catching on like a prodigy by the end of the lesson. The video is called *Does Your Dog Jump on Everyone? Here's What to Do!* Check it out to see the lesson in action. Of course, establishing proper jumping habits requires relentless consistency. But if Zeus learned when to jump appropriately, then probably any dog can.

WHAT TO DO WHEN YOUR DOG JUMPS ON YOU

Now that you understand that most dogs jump because they are just lovingly trying to engage you, let's take the mystery out of resolving this issue. Of course, a regularly exercised dog is going to be less likely to jump excessively. Also, exercising your dog just prior to these training sessions should help if your dog has a lot of energy (as many dogs who jump do!). Here's what else to do:

1. Don't wait until your dog jumps to address the issue. Instead, teach your dog not to jump by planning primary training sessions. For the first several sessions, use something that really excites your dog so that you have a way to simulate an exciting real-life situation. For example, let's say that your dog jumps relentlessly when you have a tug toy, squeaky toy, or treat in your hand. Chances are he does this because he *really* wants those items! Use this to your advantage by using those same objects as currencies during the training sessions.

2. Start by asking your dog to sit and to stay. Then, hold the toy or treat completely still above your dog's head. If your dog is super-hyper, reward for seemingly insignificant periods of time. For example, maybe your dog doesn't jump or break his stay for 1.5 seconds. Good! Say, "Yes" and reward him! Now that a good baseline has been established, let's improve on it. Work up to a ten-second stay and then maybe even a thirty-second stay over the next few training sessions.

3. As you continue these sessions, your dog may jump on you at times. If this happens, redirect him into a sit. If you notice this happening in consecutive attempts, it's best to take a step back and make the exercise easier or take a break so that you and your dog can reset and start fresh for your next training session.

4. As your dog holds his stay more and more reliably, go ahead and bring a small amount of life to the toy. Maybe move it just a little bit. Reward instantly if your dog maintains his stay and keeps

all four paws on the ground. Remember, things that move are generally more exciting to dogs than things that don't. Gradually work up to being able to move the toy more vigorously. Reward for each incremental success. If at any point you see that your dog is becoming overwhelmed or having a hard time maintaining his stay, take a step back and either move the toy a little less or take a break from training.

5. Once your dog has shown that he'll hold a stay while a toy excitedly moves around, it's time to increase the difficulty even more. Instead of the toy, it's now going to be *you* that gradually gets more exciting. So, after you ask your dog to stay, make a high-pitched sound and hop for a quick second or flap your arms. I know it sounds a bit silly, but the goal here is to work up to acting absolutely ridiculous *and* have your dog hold his stay. See, if your dog holds a stay while you make weird noises and jump off the ground, he's more likely to hold a stay and not jump on you when you come home and walk through the door.

6. Provided that your dedicated primary training sessions are going well, now set up training sessions that are more realistic but still controlled. Do this by initiating quick surprise primary training sessions. At first, grab a squeaky toy when your dog isn't expecting it, give it a squeak or two, ask your dog to sit, and reward for his compliance. [Hint: It's a good idea to have toys stashed in a place where you can quickly get to them.] At first, you may need to take a little time to ease your dog into this pop-quiz frame of mind, but as you repeat these surprise drills, your dog will likely catch on quickly and draw on his past training. Reward heavily when he does.

7. Don't limit surprise training exercises to just using toys as distractions. Work up to getting your dog to leave treats alone as you suddenly tell him to stay and start throwing treats everywhere, one at a time. What you're doing is showing your dog how to stay in the face of unpredictable, distracting events. In other words, you are teaching him to hold a rock-solid stay no matter how excited he gets or how badly he wants to move. Basic impulse

control exercises like this are what help your dog understand that he should sit and stay even in the most exciting situations.

8. Now, put everything your dog has learned into practice. Since you know your dog is likely to jump on you whenever you come in the front door, be one step ahead of him. First, when you walk in the house, don't act excited to see your dog. Instead, ignore him a bit so he can calm down and adjust to your being home. Do your best to get a brief sit and stay, and reward any success. (You might want to stash treats by the door for this very purpose.) The first many times you do this may yield minor results. This is normal. Continue to do this every time you don't want your dog to jump. If you are consistent, you should notice that your dog is more likely to sit and stay than jump when you walk in the door. It does take practice, but when it clicks, it clicks!

WHAT TO DO WHEN YOUR DOG JUMPS ON OTHERS

It's one thing to stop your dog from jumping on you, but how do you keep him from jumping on others? You've already done the hard work and laid the groundwork. Now you just need to teach your dog that the same rules apply when a real-life visitor comes over. Here's how:

1. Ideally, before your guest comes over, exercise your dog in the backyard or take him on a sufficient walk so he is less likely to want to jump excessively. Also, give your guest a heads-up that you are going to spend about five minutes showing your dog how to behave and not jump. Explain that during this training session you will be 100 percent focused on your dog, not your visitor. Of course, you can't always do this. In those cases, put your dog in another room while you let your guest in the house so that your pet can't jump. This prevents the jumping, which is an important part of management. Remember, the more a dog jumps, the more

ingrained the behavior becomes. Let your dog out once you and your guest are settled, and *then* do a brief training session (as I describe in the following points).

2. Keep your dog on leash. Ask him to sit and stay. This may take a few attempts, but remain patient and calm. You might need to be several feet away from your guest or even in an adjoining room in more extreme cases. Also, know that a common mistake during these training sessions is to ask your guests to run through these steps. That's not their job! Your dog should listen to *you* independent of what's going on around him. You've worked hard to establish a dependable communication with your dog, so now use it.

3. Once your dog is in a solid stay, give your guest permission to come over and pet him gently. For now, it's best for your guest to remain calm and neutral. At this point, a large percentage of dogs attempt to jump out of excitement. If this happens, escort your dog away and have him sit. If your dog foreshadows that he is about to break his stay at any point, again increase the distance. Your dog must know that he will receive no affection or attention from anyone unless he is honoring your request to stay. At first this may be slow going, but you'll find that once your dog learns you're going to enforce the rules, you should begin to see results here.

4. Of course, at times you or your guests might be perfectly happy having your dog jump. You can teach your dog that sometimes the behavior *is* acceptable. When you do want to allow your dog to jump on you or others, simply invite him to do so and pet and play with him to convey that jumping is fine when requested. Then feel free to let him know when you don't want him to jump anymore by following the steps we've outlined in this chapter.

CHAPTER 7

PLAY BITING

Want to know the number one thing I'm asked about? It's play biting! As precious as puppies are, anyone who has ever had one can attest— play biting hurts. A lot. Those puppy teeth might be small, but they are razor sharp!

However, play biting doesn't always end with puppyhood. In some cases, dogs well into adulthood continue this behavior. Since I work with so many untrained dogs, I film a lot of lessons with dogs who play bite excessively. As a general rule, if a dog has had little to no training, there's an excellent chance that she will play bite because she hasn't learned how to appropriately communicate with humans.

That's why it can feel like it takes forever to resolve this, because you are actually trying to accomplish two things—establishing a way to communicate with your dog *and* stopping the play biting! In this chapter, I'll help you do both of these things regardless of your dog's age.

One important note: In this chapter, I am talking about *play* biting, which is the kind of biting where a dog uses her mouth to interact with other dogs or people. However, this is extremely different from biting that's an aggressive behavior meant to cause harm. If you need help with that kind of biting, see chapter 18, which covers aggression in full detail.

WHY DO PUPPIES PLAY BITE?

Dogs are curious by nature, and they love interacting with their world and their surroundings. However, the only way a puppy can really grab things is with her mouth, which is why she play bites (also referred to as *mouthing*.) In other words, they use their mouths in the same way we use our hands. Think about asking toddlers to stop using their hands when they interact with you and imagine how unnatural that would seem to them. This is exactly what you are asking your dog to do! Dogs are not born understanding that using their mouths on us is not the acceptable way to interact with us. That's something they have to learn.

Puppy biting can also be a way for a puppy to protest or express frustration. Again, keep in mind that virtually none of this type of biting is hostile or a sign that a dog is likely to have seriously aggressive behavior. Instead, it's normal and expected for puppies to bite you as a way of saying either, "Let's play!" or "Let go of me—I don't want to be held!"

Resolving biting in puppies is fairly straightforward, but know that it can take some time to stop. Also, any time that you attempt to override an instinctive behavior, you must be extremely patient. It takes several weeks to establish clear communication with a dog, so you may have to be extra-tolerant of play biting during this "communication building" phase.

WHY DO ADULT DOGS PLAY BITE?

Some adult dogs play bite because they simply never learned not to do so when they were puppies. Others don't like to be held. In either of these cases, stopping the behavior might take longer than it would with a puppy as it is a more ingrained habit.

WHAT TO DO ABOUT PLAY BITING

It's normal for it to take days or even a few weeks just to start getting traction on reducing excessive play biting. Also, it doesn't stop all at once; instead it goes away slowly, over time. Think about it: since play biting is so natural, why would a dog stop this without being taught to stop? That's where you come in. You *can* put a stop to play biting—whether your dog is a puppy or an adult dog. Here, I'll walk you through three main ways to do just that.

Get Your Dog Used to Touch

Some dogs play bite because they get annoyed when touched or held. Usually, this is because they're not used to it. Think about it from your dog's point of view: how would you feel if you were suddenly swept up by a being many times your size and left to fend for yourself? You'd probably use any defense you could to get out of that situation. Well, that's what your dog is doing when she play bites.

So how do you desensitize your puppy to touch? Here's how:

1. Massage her around her ears, muzzle, neck, paws, and body. Since most dogs are likely to be squirmy, it's best that you start slowly and let her chew on a great chew toy to give her something fun to do.

2. You could also let her nibble on a treat that you're gripping tightly. See, if your dog is used to being touched often and even gets something good when you touch her, then she's far more likely to behave better in the future. She'll start to realize something like, "Hey, when someone gently touches my ears or my paws, I get a toy or a treat. This is awesome! I love when people touch me."

3. Of course, you'll have to repeat this drill for many weeks and as often as possible for this to sink in. Usually, older dogs aren't as sensitive to touch as they've had time to adjust to people, but you could still apply these same principles.

Recently, I shot a video with one of the most severe puppy play biters I've ever worked with. Tiberius, the Rottweiler puppy, was nine weeks old and all mouth. He was having no part of my holding him at all. His family told me that Tiberius—whose nickname is Ty—was exceptionally bitey with me as compared to with them. This was probably because I was new and unfamiliar. Also, he was in a new environment. However, I was able to improve Ty's behavior on his first lesson by desensitizing him to touch and using the other techniques I outline in this chapter. Of course, that was only the beginning, but it was a start. The video on YouTube is called *Three More Things to Teach Your New Puppy!*

Show Your Dog What's Okay to Bite

What if your dog is already a play biter? The silver lining about having a play biter on your hands is that you are in a golden position to teach tug-of-war and how to let go. Think about it: your dog wants to bite and she wants to play. The idea isn't to quell her biting all at once, but to show her when and how to bite things. That's right! One way to deal with play biting is to actually encourage it—with the proper objects, of course. So, the key is getting your dog tugging on an acceptable toy such as a rope or a plush toy with a squeaker.

This is about far more than addressing puppy biting though. A structured game of tug-of-war can also be one of the most potent currencies for your dog throughout *all* training, and there is no easier way to teach it than when a dog is already play biting. Here's a step-by-step guide:

1. At first, it's very common for a dog's interest to wax and wane when you are attempting to ignite interest in a bitable toy. For that reason, it's important to bring these tug toys to life. Give the toy movement while it's on the floor as if to make it appear to be, say, a vibrating alien squirrel from another dimension. The reason for keeping the toy on the floor is that you want your dog to easily access it. Don't give your dog a reason not to go for the toy. If it's way above her head, she might not feel like jumping up to get it.

2. If your dog pounces on the toy, play some "keep-away" but only for a second. Then let her win and grab and shake the toy while it's still in her mouth. Repeat. Let your dog win a lot in the beginning

stages of biting a new toy, and then gradually make it harder to win. This little game is a prerequisite for resolving bad play biting.

3. It's normal for this process to take many minutes or even several training sessions with an insistent biter. If you've tried extensively to trigger your dog's interest in a specific toy, and she's not interested in it, then use another one. Get creative! Sometimes the right object may not even be a toy at all. Plastic water bottles tend to be a favorite among many dogs. (Just be sure to supervise your dog, of course, so she doesn't tear the bottle to shreds.)

4. Once you find the right toy and your dog gets hooked on a game of tug, you have a huge currency in your pocket to use to redirect play biting. What's more, you can also use tug in so many other aspects of training—some dogs (like mine!) would prefer a game of tug over food as currency any day. It is true that there are some dogs who may never be interested in tug, but these guys aren't typically bad puppy biters.

5. Teaching "let go" is another critical part of teaching tug. *You* are in control of when your dog can tug and when she can't. How do you do it? Simply grip the toy tightly and make it lifeless and no fun. I'm talking a vise-like grip—you literally want your dog to feel like she is pulling on a toy stuck to a tree. Say, "Let go!" After about ten seconds to a minute, most dogs let go as the toy isn't as fun as it usually is. At this time, immediately bring the toy back to life and reward your dog with the toy as if to say, "When you let go and play by the rules, you'll get to do something fun!"

Of course, even if you are successful at getting your dog interested in a toy to tug on, she may still take turns biting the toy and your arm or hands. This is where your persistence comes in. You must continue to keep that toy interesting, bringing life and movement to it. You must also continually redirect your dog's focus to the toy. In the meantime, when play biting becomes too rough, it's fine to give your dog a quick "No" followed by removing access to your flesh or clothing in the form of a time-out. Stand up and walk a few feet away from your dog if you have to, bringing the toy with you. Over time, your dog will come to realize that excessive play biting immediately stops all fun play. Time-outs are nowhere near as effective as proactive teaching, but they may be necessary on occasion.

Teach Your Dog That Play Biting Leads to Training

Of course, you may not want to redirect your dog into a play session every time she seems like she's in a biting mood. And at times, it makes sense to keep her energy dialed down a little rather than throttling it up by playing with her. Sounds like a secondary training session is in order! Here's what you can do:

1. If your dog is getting bitey, grab one of those soft, room tempera-ture dog treats from a sealed bag or container. At this point, your dog will likely stop biting and go into a sit. Great! You've got her where you want her. (If she doesn't sit, then check out page 46, chapter 3, for a refresher on how to teach this skill.)

2. Next, initiate a simple training session centered around things you've already taught her, such as "down," "come," and "stay." This approach has a great way of changing a dog's focus from biting to training. If you consistently redirect your dog's interest from playing to a basic training session, then she'll have no choice but to learn that biting doesn't work for her.

3. Changing the mood from playtime to a more formal training session has two massive benefits to teaching a dog not to play bite. First, she'll likely be in a much more cooperative mind-set now that food has been brought out. Provided you are consistent, she ought to learn very quickly that biting you does not result in her getting her treat. Secondly, most dogs bite significantly less by default when in food mode versus play mode. Some signs that you are on the right track are when your dog starts biting less and licking those areas where the biting used to occur.

Bottom line: If your dog play bites, you have two major options—redirect her attention to a toy to play tug with or initiate a basic training session to get her mind off of vigorous play. Of course, you can and should use a combination of the two in your training. And remember—if your dog is biting specifically because she's not used to people handling her, then it's time to desensitize her to touch.

If you are occasionally unable or unwilling to engage your dog at any moment, unless she's playing biting you can place her in another room until she calms down a bit. However, you'll need to be proactive most of the time so that such time-outs don't become a long-term solution.

Of course, it's extra-critical to control whom your dog has access to as you want to do your best to guarantee that your dog doesn't bite another person, even if playfully. If you're around other people, especially kids, keep your dog on leash until her play biting is completely under control.

CHAPTER 8

POTTY PROBLEMS

Potty training is one of those things that can take longer than you might expect. It can take months to fully accomplish, though the overall time varies with each dog. Needless to say, you've got to stay patient and overwhelmingly consistent.

If you need a refresher step-by-step on how to potty train your dog, check out my various YouTube videos on the subject. (Start with *How to Potty Train Your Puppy Easily! Everything You Need to Know!*) Also, my first book, *Zak George's Dog Training Revolution*, goes over potty training in great depth.

However, plenty of people go through the steps and still have trouble with potty training. Others have perfectly potty-trained dogs for years who suddenly, out of the blue, start having accidents in the house again. Whether your dog is having a slow start or experiencing relapses, you *can* get things under control.

This chapter helps you with these issues.

WHY DO DOGS SOMETIMES NOT "GET" POTTY TRAINING?

If your dog is having a tough time getting the picture with potty training, it has nothing to do with his intelligence. Instead, it's just an issue of basic biology: Dogs do not intuitively understand where they're supposed to go potty. To them, it's just as normal and natural to make inside as it is to make outside. We have to teach them how to go potty on *our* terms.

The number one reason people have a hard time with potty training is that they greatly underestimate how important it is to control their dog's environment. Seriously! You cannot let your dog have access to any part of the house he pleases if he is having regular accidents in those areas. Doing so just makes potty-training progress nearly impossible.

Also, you might notice that your dog tends to have accidents in pretty consistent parts of the house. Typically, dogs do not do their business in areas they view as their "home." You might be wondering how your dog could possibly not view your entire residence as his home. Well, it seems that dogs don't generalize well from room to room or area to area within the house. While your living room and bedroom might feel like home to your pet, for instance, the dining room and guest room might not. But we'll work on that!

What if your dog sniffs around forever while on walks, doesn't make, and then sneaks off and poops in the house once he's back home? Again, this is most likely due to the fact that he simply has not yet learned that going outside is the preferred place to go. (It's certainly not because he's stubborn or spiteful as I explained on page 33, chapter 2.)

WHAT TO DO ABOUT POTTY TRAINING DELAYS

Just as toddlers have to learn to use a potty, dogs need to learn they should only make outside. However, while some dogs seem to understand this concept right away, others take some time. Here are some tips that will help speed up the process:

1. First and foremost, get control of the environment. Do this even if it means taking a big step back and attaching your dog to you with his leash while inside the house. Remember, you have to first put a stop to unwanted behaviors by making it impossible for them to occur. In this case, your dog cannot sneak off to the upstairs guest room if he is on leash. If you are easily able to contain your dog in an area of the house where accidents are not occurring—say, in your family room or kitchen—this may also be a sufficient way to control your dog's environment. You might also want to use your dog's crate or a playpen to contain him when you can't watch him or when you're away from the house. Once you've regained control of your dog's environment, only now are you in a position to teach.

2. Go back to basics. It's on you to let your dog outside very regularly, about every hour or so, whether you think he has to go or not. Training is about racking up consecutive successes, so the more you take your dog outside, the more likely he'll successfully go potty where he is supposed to do so. Your goal is to help him create a new habit.

3. Whenever your dog does his business in a place that you approve of, generously reward him with a great treat right then and there. Or if your dog is the more playful type, go from boring to super-fun once he's done. Make a huge fuss and say, "Good dog!" in a high-pitched voice, for example. The logic here is that you are providing a positive outcome that, in time, he comes to associate with peeing or pooping in acceptable areas. This is what reinforcement training is all about!

4. If your dog is only making in certain parts of the house, work on training your dog to specifically not go potty in those areas. In other words, your dog would need to hang out in those rooms under strict supervision for sustained periods of time over the course of weeks or even longer. The more time he spends in a room without going potty in it, the less likely he is to have an accident there. If your dog is making in the room while you're there, then take him out more often.

5. Avoid a super-common rookie mistake for new pet parents: expecting your dog to let you know when he wants to go outside. Instead, it's your job to get your dog outside often and consistently for the next several months to really ingrain this habit. Sure, you can teach your dog to ring a bell attached to your door and pair that with letting your dog outside. And yes, your dog may correlate, "Hey, ringing the bell gets me outside." There's no harm in teaching this for *potty-trained dogs*. In fact, I have a great video with Sky Blue, a prodigy Lab, on how to do just this, called *Potty Training: How to Train Your Dog to Ring a Bell to Be Let Outside*. Sky Blue was a champ and actually learned this skill in a single lesson. However, this is not a reliable way to potty train a dog—it's for dogs who are already reliably making outside. Also, don't be surprised if your dog starts ringing the bell *many* times in the day just to go outside and play!

6. If your dog has issues with potty training because he seemingly can't stand the thought of going outside or, in particular, touching grass, work on this issue. Spend some training sessions getting your dog comfortable walking on grass or other surfaces he might not like, independent of potty breaks. For example, bring some chicken out with you and toss a bit just over the threshold where the sidewalk or asphalt meets the grass. See if you can get your dog to put one foot on the grass and make progress from there. It can take time, but the more often your dog spends time on grass, the less likely it is to cause him angst. However, keep in mind that progress is unlikely if you consistently wait until you are on actual potty breaks with your dog to work on this because you are attempting to teach two things simultaneously: walking on a surface your dog doesn't like *and* potty training. Instead, set up primary training sessions specifically about getting your dog comfortable on grass ahead of time! In the meantime, you might try picking up your dog and setting him on the grass, provided he's not extremely anxious about it. Of course, this won't teach him much, but it may help desensitize him a little, which could have some benefit.

7. When your dog does have accidents in the house, remember you should never punish him. That's like punishing a baby for going in his diaper! Yelling at your dog won't teach him anything; all it does is hurt your bond. The best course of action is to up your game when it comes to controlling his environment and letting him out more often. If you do catch your dog in the act, quickly pick him up or escort him outside if you're not too late. Also, be sure to thoroughly clean up any accidents that do occur. Dogs have extremely sensitive noses, and the smell of urine can stimulate their urge to repeat the behavior in the same area. Choose an enzyme-based cleaner that neutralizes the odor.

8. If you want to use potty pads, follow the same steps I've outlined, but instead of walking your dog outside you'll walk him directly to the potty pads. You'll still need to control the environment and be consistent about taking your dog to the pads. Where you keep the pads is up to you: if you'd like to put them out just prior to your dog's potty break, that's fine. If you'd like to keep them out all the time, that's fine, too. However, note that if your ultimate goal is to get your dog making outside, then I wouldn't recommend using potty pads in the interim—it's an unnecessary step and might confuse your dog. Only use potty pads if you *always* plan on using them.

HANDLING SETBACKS

I can't tell you how many times people come to me saying things like, "My dog was perfectly potty trained, but now he's having accidents in the house again. What should I do?" Well, the first thing I say is that they are certainly not alone. Potty-training setbacks—which is when your dog has demonstrated that he's potty trained but then suddenly starts making in the house again—occur for all sorts of reasons. For instance, when it comes to potty training, it's common for people to assume victory prematurely and let their guard down too soon. However, training is about extensive follow-through for months and months. Without it, your dog can quickly lose a lot of the progress he's made. Here are some other reasons your dog might experience setbacks and what to do about them:

- Certain medical issues, ranging from a urinary tract infection to diabetes, can suddenly make a dog have to go to the bathroom more frequently *and* with little notice. So, if your dog is having setbacks, first things first: schedule a vet visit.

- If you have a new baby or roommate or you've changed your dog's routine in any other way, he might experience setbacks. That's because it doesn't take much to throw some dogs off with potty training. In these cases, slow down and go back to the basics. Be patient—your dog will get back on track. He just needs some time to adjust to the new variable.

- A change in environment can also cause a dog to have major setbacks. Most dogs do not generalize new places well—they might understand that they shouldn't go potty in your home, but that doesn't mean they understand that they shouldn't go in other places. So, if you've moved recently, if you're leaving your dog at a sitter's home, or you're just visiting a friend's house for the day, your dog might want to investigate these new, fun places to relieve himself. In these cases, keep your dog on a leash or under very strict supervision no matter how well he was potty trained before. He'll have to learn where he can and cannot go potty in this new environment. The good news is that it shouldn't take long if he caught on before. In fact, a quick walk or two outside where you reward your dog for going on the grass can do the trick.

HANDLING EXCITEMENT URINATION/ SUBMISSIVE URINATION

Excitement urination is when your dog is overcome with joy and just starts involuntarily peeing anywhere and everywhere. *Submissive urination* is when dogs, especially young ones and/or those who aren't socialized, involuntarily pee when seeing a new person or dog or when someone becomes upset with them. These behaviors are both particularly common among dogs under eighteen months or so, and they often diminish over time as dogs mature. Socializing a dog at a young age and desensitizing him to people or situations likely to cause him to become excited or nervous should speed up your progress.

If your dog has excitement urination, discourage guests from interacting with him until he settles down. When you come home, you should do the same! Don't get your dog all riled up and start playing fetch. Instead, whisk him right outside.

If your dog pees out of nervousness when in a new place such as a vet's office or a friend's house, this is your cue to do some environmental desensitizing. Make it a priority to set up time to slowly introduce your dog to these new places in positive ways. You might spend ten to thirty minutes in front of the vet's office or your friend's house just hanging out or doing some easy training. Use your dog's favorite currency here! As your dog becomes more relaxed, you can consider going inside at that point.

With both excitement and submissive urination, it always helps to take your dog outside right before guests come over or before any activity that might cause your dog to pee inside.

CHAPTER 9

LEASH PULLING

We all have to walk our dogs several times every day. However, that's often a lot easier said than done. I cover many behavioral issues in my YouTube videos on the top, but year after year, leash pulling remains one of the most popular topics. (Check out my leash walking playlist on YouTube to see my videos on the topic all in one place.)

In this chapter, I'll teach you how to walk your dog properly and how to get any lunging, pulling, leash biting, and other inappropriate leash behaviors under control.

WHY DO DOGS PULL ON LEASHES?

Dogs pull on leashes for lots of reasons. For one, they naturally walk significantly faster than we do. It's not easy for a dog to slow her natural pace when doing something as basic as walking. In fact, this skill is more advanced than you might realize. Also, dogs have their own reasons for enjoying a walk that we often don't consider. You might want your dog to do her business outside quickly, but she'd rather take her time to figure out where certain cool smells are coming from, to investigate something fascinating she sees in the grass, or to chase after the squirrel that just ran up the tree.

WHAT TO DO ABOUT LEASH PULLING

There are two main steps you need to take to resolve most types of leash pulling. Here's an overview of both.

Step #1
First, your dog must have an outlet for all of her energy. It stands to reason that if your dog is lying around all day, bored out of her mind, with no way to exercise, then when you do take her out on a walk she is going to be *bursting* with energy. The key is to make sure she gets enough exercise during the day so that walks are much more manageable. As I've mentioned throughout this book, fetch is a perfect option.

Exercise has an added bonus when it comes to training: one of the absolute best times to do a leash training session is instantly after a workout that tires your dog—the kind where she's so wiped out that she couldn't run if she wanted to. While you're not exactly proactively training your dog to walk slowly next to you on leash since she's too tired to walk fast anyway, she *is* experiencing what you would like the walk to be like: walking at a normal, enjoyable pace for both of you. It also allows her to take in the environment and everything it has to offer while she is too tired to go crazy over it. This goes so far toward desensitizing your dog to a stimulating outdoor environment. The more instances in which you can create good behavior, even if your dog is fatigued from a long workout, the more it helps her progress.

However, I also know that this isn't always practical. If you live in an urban environment, you might have to walk your dog to the park in order to play some fetch. Or maybe you've been trying for months to get your dog interested in fetch and other activities, but walking is the only reliable way you can currently get her energy out.

So, you have another option: take her for a long enough walk that she expends enough energy to then focus on learning proper leash walking. For instance, your dog may need to walk briskly for up to twenty minutes before settling down a bit. I understand this is somewhat counterintuitive to my other training advice. However, if you have a dog who pulls, and you are unable to exercise her *before* leash training, then you really just have to wait for her to tire a bit during the walk.

Step #2

So what's the second step you need to take? You've got to normalize the exciting environment your dog encounters on walks. You do this through frequent exposure and desensitization drills so that the smells, sights, and sounds aren't a special occasion anymore. And you do that by teaching proper leash walking! Here's how:

1. Throughout this training, use high-value rewards. Also, make sure that you train in an environment where your dog listens. For example, your first training lessons should take place inside your home where your dog is comfortable. You can gradually make the environment more challenging as long as you make sure your dog is always in a trainable mind-set. How do you do this? It's essential that you measure her compliance often by asking for a "sit" and a "look at me." If your dog does not reliably honor such requests, this is a great sign that the environment you're teaching in is too distracting.

2. Start by walking around inside with your dog on a leash. Take a few steps and ask your dog to sit. Generously reward when she does. Do you see what we're doing here? You are breaking training down into small, manageable segments. At no point should any next step be hard for your dog. For many of you, this may be the first time you've ever seen your dog behave on leash!

3. As you perfect these lessons in your house, practice those surprise primary lessons, too. Out of nowhere, put the leash on your dog and quickly jump into an indoor leash training session. By doing this, you are teaching your dog that even when she's caught off guard, she still needs to comply.

4. As your dog becomes proficient with these lessons, set up random, unpredictable distractions. Maybe you throw a treat or a toy in front of your dog, for example, and then request a "leave it/look at me." The idea is to work up to being able to distract your dog as much as possible in this easy, indoor environment before moving on. See, if your dog cannot pay attention to you on leash while in your living room, then there's no reason to believe that she'll be able to handle a sudden surprise on a real walk, such as a group of kids whizzing by on bicycles. If at any point the training seems too daunting to your dog, immediately take a step back and make the exercises easier.

5. Now, it's time to do these identical lessons in your driveway or right in front of your front door. Follow the same drill that you did indoors. These walking lessons should cover a range of five to twenty yards in length back and forth, up and down, in figure eights and other random patterns. The only goal here is to make sure that your dog is keeping up with you as you suddenly change course frequently.

6. Since you are outside now, you are also likelier to encounter more distractions. For example, there are lots of smells. Also, your dog might hear other dogs barking in the distance, or she might encounter a stray cat or a bird. If at any point you do encounter a distraction that causes your dog to pull on her leash and become too distracted to pay attention to you, promptly create distance between your dog and the distraction. Even go back inside if necessary. The farther away the distraction is, the more likely your dog is to listen to you. How do you know when you are far enough away? Again, measure! When you ask your dog for a "sit" and a "look at me," and she complies and doesn't pull, you're at the right spot. As you get to know your dog throughout this training, you should have a good baseline for how far something needs to be from your dog before you have her attention.

7. Once you've done this long enough for your dog to reliably focus on you, usually over a few dozen lessons, it's time to do a training walk. However, this still isn't a proper, leisurely walk as you

should still be completely focused on your dog and any potential distractions. At this point, escort your dog up and down the street. As you cover more and more new territory in your neighborhood, your dog might lose focus at times. What is your course of action when your dog becomes distracted and starts pulling on her leash suddenly? Measure! Create enough distance until you can get a reliable "sit" and "look at me."

8. Assuming you go out of your way to do these training sessions, you and your dog will be much more prepared to handle distractions while on actual walks. Don't become complacent, however. Leash training usually takes extensive follow-through for a solid year at least or you risk regression! Keep up with the indoor and outdoor training, and don't forget to bring high-currency treats on walks so you can randomly reinforce good behavior for those unplanned secondary training sessions (training that occurs spontaneously in real life as opposed to training that you planned) that require quick action on your part.

HANDLING LEASH REACTIVITY

Let's talk about those dogs who tend to react excessively to other dogs, people, or animals while walking. For instance, when your dog acts out and starts lunging and barking at another dog on a walk, it could be that she is so happy to see that dog that she can't contain her excitement. Or it could be that she is suddenly thrown off by this dog, and she wants to engage the dog in a more dangerous or inappropriate way. You'll need to do your best to identify the underlying cause.

If you think it's the latter cause, then you might ask why a dog would act aggressively while on leash. In a nutshell: Dogs feel trapped. "When dogs are off leash, they have the ability to create space when around other dogs as they first determine how their interactions will progress," explains John Ciribassi, DVM, DACVB, past president of the American Veterinary Society of Animal Behavior and coeditor of the book *Decoding Your Dog*.[1] "In using nonverbal communications such as tail position, head position, and eye contact, dogs can get a good idea of each other's intentions and make a decision regarding whether or not they want to interact with another dog. A leash prevents this type of communication and also prevents the dog's ability to create space. This, in turn, makes her feel more vulnerable."

Of course, you need to walk your dog on a leash, so what do you do? When it comes to handling leash reactivity, there are two major issues you need to address: leash pulling *and* overreacting to something. So, you've got to work on both (after making sure your dog is getting enough exercise, of course!). If your dog is unpleasantly reactive to, say, other dogs when she encounters them on a walk, you'll need to go do some extra desensitizing and counterconditioning along with the proper leash walking drills I outlined earlier in this chapter.

For example, let's say there's one street that you avoid going down because there's a loud dog who starts barking at you and your dog through a fence. And let's say your dog starts barking and pulling like crazy as you get close to passing the dog. In this case, plan on doing a primary training session about five houses away from this dog—far enough away where you can still get a "sit" and a "look at me." Your goal is to find that spot where your dog goes from not listening to you to likely to listen to you so that you'll know what your workable distance is.

Once you identify this distance, work on gradually being able to gain compliance at closer and closer distances. These counterconditioning exercises might simply be taking three steps in the direction of the barking dog and then giving a treat to your dog over and over again. You are attempting to change the way your dog reacts in this situation. Whereas before, she would bark, now she eagerly pays attention to you. It's normal for this to take dozens of training sessions in this particular situation.

What if your dog reacts excessively when she sees *any* other dog or person while on a walk? Again, you'll need to take a step back and do some desensitization work. In other words, it's not reasonable to expect results here until you've set up primary training sessions and surprise primary training sessions for your dog where you are in complete control of the variables. So, if your dog is highly reactive on neighborhood walks, then first know she's not yet ready for casual walks in the neighborhood. Set up training lessons in areas where your dog is more likely to be in a teachable mind-set—say, on a dead-end street where you know there are no dogs in the vicinity or maybe early in the morning before your neighbors take their dogs on walks. You could even sit on your driveway or front porch and practice "look at me" while the other dogs walk by.

When it comes time to test to see if your dog willingly complies, you need to be prepared for a couple of scenarios. If your dog's concentration is broken and she begins to react unfavorably, immediately escort her away from the other dog or person until her distraction level has subsided enough to sit and look at you. However, if your dog is showing more restraint than before, even if minimal, reward her with her favorite currency. See chapter 19 on listening with distractions for more information on how to help your dog react calmly no matter what she sees on a walk.

HANDLING LEASH BITING

Sometimes dogs are so excited and worked up about being on a walk that they start biting on the leash. Think about this from their perspective: they might be thinking, "There's a dangling, skinny, wiggly, bitable thing very close to me!" This is most common with puppies, but lots of playful older dogs do this, too. I actually love this issue. It's almost always about a dog screaming, "Let's play! Let's interact! Let's do something fun!" See, to me this is the most ideal frame of mind for a dog to be in when it comes to teaching her because you can reward her with playtime. I know the behavior itself is obnoxious, but the mind-set is great!

How should you handle this? You can try to redirect your dog's attention from a leash to a tug rope or other tug toy. Your goal is to make the tug toy very enticing and exciting, moving it around on the ground or right in front of your dog's face. It's normal for your dog to be a little distracted and to go back and forth between the toy and the leash at first. However, be persistent about redirecting her to the appropriate toy—eventually, your dog will learn that when she bites on the tug toy instead of her leash, life is more fun because there's someone on the other end of the toy, purposely pulling it, trying to engage her in an exciting game. For most dogs, this is ultimately more gratifying than biting the leash and constantly being redirected.

If your dog still seems to think, "No, I still want to play with the leash" and continues biting at the leash for whatever reason, a simple training exercise is in order. Just place a treat at her nose and request a "sit" and a "look at me." Treat for compliance no matter how small at first. Yes, you're going to have to do this a lot initially—this process can take days, even weeks. Like anything, generously reward in the beginning stages.

HANDLING A DOG WHO FREEZES UP ON A LEASH

Some dogs might have the opposite issue of pulling on a leash. Instead, they freeze up and become dead weight. In most cases, this is because a dog is not used to being on leash, so just be patient and dedicate some primary training sessions to luring her back and forth with a treat while she's on leash. Also, let her walk around your house with the leash hanging and just get her used to wearing it. For a visual lesson on how to do this, check out my YouTube video with BB-8, the Alaskan Klee Kai, *How to Teach Your New Puppy to Walk on Leash!*

However, sometimes dogs freeze up on their leashes because of something causing them anxiety. For example, some may freeze up when the surface beneath their feet changes from concrete to grass. Or they may freeze up when approaching something making a loud sound.

As with virtually all training, don't wait until you are confronted with your dog becoming uncooperative to then try to overcome this. Instead, be proactive and set up dedicated training sessions for these issues.

For instance, let's say your dog freezes up when walking on grass, as might be the case for some city dogs. Be sure to spend significant time hanging out near a grassy area so that your dog gets more familiar with the grass nearby. First, work on your general leash training with lots of treats or playtime on the sidewalk *near* the grass. This helps your dog develop a positive association of being near the grass. Then, as your dog adapts to the environment, attempt to lure her onto the grass. If she seems to so much as think about stepping on the grass, generously reward her. The magic moment here is when your dog places one paw on the grass.

At first you may meet resistance with this, but that's okay. It's really important to go slowly if your dog is afraid of something. You may make little progress in your first couple of training sessions, but if you remain patient and understanding, you ought to steadily see improvement. See chapter 15 for more information on dealing with issues that make your dog fearful.

TEACHING MULTIPLE DOGS PROPER LEASH WALKING

Even if you have more than one dog, you need to teach each of your pets proper leash walking one-on-one first. Yes, this means leaving one dog inside while you take the other one out for training.

Why must you train them separately? Whereas before, you set up distractions like randomly throwing a treat or toy to test your dog, now you are adding a more significant distraction: another dog who just might be her best friend! Also, dogs are particularly quick to note when your attention is divided.

Once you've taught each dog to walk well while alone on leash, the process of getting them to walk well together should be pretty smooth sailing. The steps are the same; now you're just doing the training sessions with multiple dogs instead of one. For instance, you'd teach two or more dogs to walk acceptably *while together* from inside your residence, then in front of it, and then while walking up and down the street nearest your home. However, if you run into difficulty, you might need to just take a step back in order to reteach some aspects of leash training to each dog independently. In general, teaching multiple dogs to walk nicely together requires a combination of frequently occurring lessons with the dogs apart and then gradually with them together.

SPECIAL COLLARS AND OTHER SUPPLIES
FOR LEASH WALKING

Do: Basket Muzzles. Training in public requires you to be prepared for handling situations where you encounter other dogs, other animals, small children, or other people. It's pretty much impossible to always strictly control the environment when you are in public. If you are unsure as to how your dog might react in these situations, it might be a good idea to condition her to enjoy wearing a basket muzzle. In fact, I think all dogs should at least learn to love wearing a muzzle just in case you ever need to use one. Basket muzzles are the most humane muzzles I've come across. They still allow dogs to pant, drink, and receive treats while preventing them from being able to bite should an unforeseen circumstance arise. Of course, don't leave your dog in a basket muzzle for longer than necessary and never put her in one unsupervised. Check out my video *How and Why Every Dog Should Love Wearing a Muzzle* to learn how to properly put a basket muzzle on your dog and use it appropriately.

Don't: Choke, Prong, or Electric Collars. By now you might be asking yourself why not just use a training collar like a choke, prong, or electric collar? After all, if you use these devices "correctly" by providing a rapid, harsh "pop" of the collar when leash pulling occurs, then a dog is likely to stop pulling. However, I really advise against using these devices. First, they can hurt your dog. Second, there's no way to harm your relationship with your pet faster than by causing her pain. It's critical to the training process that you keep your dog in an optimistic, fun state of mind as much as possible because this contributes to a bond and willingness to learn like nothing else. Also, even though these devices might help with leash walking as they provide a highly unpleasant consequence to pulling, they are just a bandage, not a solution. In other words, they are the epitome of outside-in training: at best, your dog learns not to pull because you are going to provide a painful punishment, not because she is generalizing how to behave in a variety of environments and contexts.

CHAPTER 10

BEGGING AND OTHER PUSHY BEHAVIORS

Begging and constant attention seeking drive *a lot* of people crazy. You've probably experienced such behavior at one point or another. You know, when your dog just stares at you, insisting that you drop a scrap of food on the floor or stop what you're doing to give him a belly rub. Of course, there are times when we just want our dogs to calm down and give us some space. Maybe you have company over or maybe you just want to eat dinner without your dog making you feel *really* guilty that you're not sharing it with him.

If you watch my videos, you're probably familiar with Jacob, an adorable Pit Bull–mix rescue dog. Jacob's quick backstory is that he was up for adoption at a shelter in New Orleans, where I live. At the same time, I was looking for a dog who had zero training but lots of energy for a video I wanted to make for my YouTube channel. I was purposefully looking for a challenging dog, and Jacob was perfect for the job! He was as wild and spirited as a dog can be—a proper high-energy dog who was far from trained. He was about a year old and seventy pounds of pure muscle. Long story short, my wife's dad, Mike, fell in love with Jacob upon meeting him and adopted him on the spot. Jacob became great material for a whole series of videos that we ended up producing, and Mike and I certainly had a lot of fun training him together! I'm reminded what an amazing dog he is every time I see him.

One of the videos I made with Jacob was called *How to Train Your Dog to Stop Begging and Settle Down*, and it's one of my favorite training videos I've ever made. Jacob wasn't just a beggar for food—he *demanded* attention at all times. Watch the video—at first Jacob was so relentless with his need for my attention, it's a miracle I was able to film it. However, I eventually got this loving, pushy dog to really calm down. In this chapter, I'll teach you how you can do that with your dog, too.

WHY DO DOGS BEG AND DEMAND ATTENTION?

It's easy for this behavior to become well established early because all it takes is feeding your dog a couple of times while you're eating something for him to always start expecting you to share. Also, many dogs are opportunists and seek attention and engagement from anyone and everyone. If that behavior goes unchecked, it'll just continue. Reversing this established bad habit can be a bit more challenging than preventing it in the first place, but it's doable!

WHAT TO DO ABOUT BEGGING AND OTHER PUSHY BEHAVIORS

Resolving behaviors like begging and pushiness comes down to showing your dog how you'd prefer he'd behave instead. Not only do we want our dogs to stop being so insistent for attention or food, but we also want to teach them how to settle down and tune out, too. In other words, teaching your dog "settle" is your way of telling your dog, "Calm down. I'm busy right now." And it's the key for resolving these particular behaviors.

Believe me, teaching this skill really comes in handy! I can remember many times being at the park with my Border Collies playing Frisbee over the years. It was great to be able to tell them, "Settle please" and have them behave any time I needed a break or wanted to talk to someone.

There are some significant prerequisites to teaching "settle." Your dog must know a reliable "down" and "stay"—so reliable that you are past giving him a reward every time he does those things. See pages 46 and 51, chapter 3, for a refresher on these skills. Also, check out my YouTube video *How to Get Your Dog to Listen Without Treats* for an illustration of how to wean your dog off treats over time. Chapter 22 covers the topic in depth, too.

The reason a "down" and a "stay" without a food reward is vital here is that your dog needs to have generalized these skills for many minutes at a time in day-to-day life. Also, rewarding your dog with food while teaching him not to beg for food might be a bit confusing.

Throughout this particular training, the idea is to keep your dog in a calm, relaxed mood. Also, we won't wait until the begging or pushiness organically occurs to address this. You must set up training scenarios that mimic real life if you are to truly prepare your dog. Teaching "settle" is a slow process since it's not so much a physical position you're teaching as it is a relaxed state of mind. By waiting until your actual mealtime or when you have guests over, your attention is likely to be divided and your dog might become way too riled up. You can't teach that way! Maximize your training time when things are calm and free of major distractions.

Lastly, if your dog happens to be high-energy like Jacob is, then exercise just before these primary training sessions is *critical*. It also helps if your dog has a full stomach during these sessions if begging is his particular issue—if he's extra-hungry, it makes sense that he'll more likely beg for food. So, let's teach your dog "settle."

Settle

A textbook "settle" is where a dog lies down and tunes out. He's not anticipating additional instructions from you as he might in a more formal "down" or a "stay." Instead, he just chill outs and relaxes—he can even take a nap! Just keep in mind that this is a more advanced skill that does require some maturity, so don't expect a three-month-old hyper puppy to catch on to this one! Usually, a dog can learn "settle" once he has a strong grasp of basic skills, which can take a few months of training.

1. Start your "settle" training sessions when your dog is at his most low-key and relaxed—maybe after a long walk or game of fetch. "Settle" should mean "lie down, stay, and relax until further notice." As your dog holds his stay, pet him softly and say, "Settle." Remain calm and relaxed yourself, too—your dog picks up on your mood! You likely need to do this over several sessions for your dog to begin to understand what "settle" means. Prioritize teaching this while you're watching TV or doing other low-key activities around the house.

2. Another ideal time to teach a good "settle" is when your dog is already doing it naturally. This is called *capturing* a behavior. Say "Settle" any time your dog begins to lie down and relax on his own. This way you're introducing the term very clearly. This takes dozens of repetitions over time, but dogs do catch on to what these requests mean when introduced contextually.

3. Once you think your dog understands "settle," set up a five- to ten-minute training session that specifically teaches him to settle during mealtime. Call or escort your dog over to his bed or other area where he's likely to be comfortable and ask him to settle. For now, it's best for your dog to remain in sight. Be patient! When your dog seems to relax momentarily, subtly acknowledge his success and go back to the table. You might softly say, "Good boy, thank you for settling." Sit at the table with food in front of you—it can be anything your dog might want (which, if your dogs are anything like mine, is pretty much everything!). If your dog breaks his "settle" at any time, calmly escort him back to his spot and repeat the drill as necessary. If you notice that your dog is just too

excited and not complying, then take a step back. Maybe you need to go back to teaching "settle" a little better or perhaps you're just asking him to settle for too long. Remember, small steps lead to faster progress.

4. Now that you've addressed begging during training, up the ante. Maybe you can have more people sitting at the table or even include more varieties of tempting foods. You can also stay at the table longer—work from five to ten minutes of simulated training up to thirty minutes or longer at a real meal (as long as you're willing to snap into training mode during mealtime). Plus, you can start addressing other pushy behaviors, like when you have company over and your dog is insisting they pay attention to him. Or maybe you're with your dog at a friend's house, and you want him to settle while you enjoy your visit. The good news is you can handle those other pushy behaviors in the *same exact way* you handle begging.

5. A big part of teaching dogs is keeping instances of unwanted behavior from occurring at all if possible, or at least greatly minimizing them. There may be times where teaching your dog not to beg or be pushy is less practical for one reason or another. Maybe, for instance, you're in a hurry to finish breakfast because you're running behind. Or perhaps you're having a party at your house, and the excitement is too much for your dog. You just might not have time to ask your dog to settle and make sure he remains in that position. In that case, it's best to put your dog in another room so that he doesn't even have an opportunity to beg. That way, at least, your dog is not falling back into the pushy behavior.

6. There's no harm in rewarding your dog *after* you are done eating or after your dog has held a nice settle while company is over. However, these rewards should be given nonchalantly as if to say, "Thank you for behaving nicely." Teaching "settle" to my own dogs taught me that dogs really can understand these nuanced concepts.

CHAPTER 11

STEALING

If left to their own devices, dogs are usually major opportunists! For instance, if your dog sees something interesting, like your lunch or even your phone on the coffee table, she might grab it and do what she wants with it if you haven't taught her how to handle these types of temptations. It's on us to make sure we train our dogs how not to steal things—or to stop doing so if they've already picked up the bad habit. Either way, I'll teach you how to get this under control.

WHY DO DOGS STEAL?

Dogs steal things for several reasons. Of course, it's pretty obvious why your dog might try to steal the meatball sub or chicken drumstick you left sitting out on the kitchen counter. She wants to devour every single morsel! Also, dogs are curious creatures, and they might steal something simply because they want to investigate it further.

WHAT TO DO ABOUT STEALING

I've taught many dogs, including my own, to not touch a plate of food I leave on the floor. I know that might seem impossible, but I promise you, it's not that difficult. Here's a step-by-step guide on how to get your dog to stop stealing:

1. The first step is to make it virtually impossible for your dog to steal. By doing so, you manage your dog's behavior and bring the habit to a standstill (or, better yet, prevent it from occurring in the first place). This is done by limiting your dog's access to things that might tempt her by keeping her on leash and attached to you. If you rely on a strategy of trying to rush to your dog and interrupt a "theft" in progress, you'll almost certainly be too late most of the time to actually teach her.

2. Next, plan a primary training session. You first need to teach your dog a solid "leave it," which I cover on page 47, chapter 3. Then, continue teaching her "leave it" in a variety of situations that resemble real-life circumstances over the coming weeks. Tempt your dog with various foods and other objects. The video *How to Teach Your Puppy to Actually Listen to You When It Counts! (Real-Life "Leave It" Explained!)* teaches this really well. The dog in that specific video, Izzy, was very young, yet she excelled at this concept. It really only takes a training session or two to get traction on this skill.

3. Next, add, "look at me" to the mix (I teach "leave it/look at me" on page 49, chapter 3). This combo is a fundamental training step for impulse control exercises. In short, it's where you ask your dog to leave something alone that she wants and to look at you instead. When you have your dog's eyes voluntarily, you can communicate amazingly well! Remember, these are still primary training sessions. You are not waiting for your dog to slip up. Rather, you are proactively preparing her for actual instances that are likely to occur in the future.

4. Need help visualizing this drill? Here's an example: Maybe you're in the kitchen and you have dinner in the oven. While you wait for your meal to cook, go ahead and place a temptation right on the counter or low table within your dog's reach. Maybe you have a scrap of food nearby, like some vegetables or other snack. Choose something tempting and make sure your dog sees the food and where you put it. Perhaps even place it beneath her nose for a split second as if to say, "I want you to know what this is and where it is! But I want you to leave it alone." Say, "Leave it." Then, calmly ask for your dog's attention by saying, "Look at me." Do this to confirm that you have your dog's willing compliance.

5. If your dog doesn't steal the food, then reward her liberally with consecutive tiny treats. The *rate of reinforcement* is particularly key at first, so rapidly give three to five small treats every second for the first few successes here to help make the point to your dog that *not* stealing gets her lots of rewards. You can use a small piece of the actual food distraction (assuming it's safe for your dog to eat). However, if you do so, pick it up and give it to your dog so that she associates the reward as coming directly from you. You may also use separate treats instead.

6. If at any time your dog goes for the food, just block access to it with your body or hand, place or lure her into a sit, and ask for a "look at me." Reward your dog when she complies. This is inside-out training! Try to avoid pulling her away as that does not teach your dog to think and reason through her actions. If you pull her away, she's learning nothing and the next time there's food on the counter, she might think something like, "No one is here to pull me away from the food. I'll bet I can get it before they get to me!" Dogs are excellent opportunists!

7. If your dog keeps going for the food during an exercise, then the next time make the session easier by either insisting that your dog leave the temptation alone for a shorter period of time or making the decoy something less interesting (i.e., probably *not* a pot roast). Once you gain some traction, pick up the pace a bit. Instead of dropping, say, one carrot on the floor, drop several.

Or drop various objects. Or ask your dog to leave the food for longer. Remember, the more instances your dog listens to you in realistic practice, the more likely she is to listen in real life.

8. After you feel your dog is getting the concept of not stealing over several training sessions, it's time to teach your dog how to leave things alone when you are not looking and even when you are out of the room. Start by turning your back and then repeat the exercise I just outlined. You are literally trying to make your dog *think* that you are no longer paying attention. However, be sure to watch her out of the corner of your eye. Every little change is likely to throw your dog off—and in this case, the changed variable is that you're no longer obviously watching her. Therefore, assume she is likely to struggle at first. Go very slowly and reward generously for preliminary success. That could mean just a few seconds of your dog leaving something alone while your back is turned.

9. Over the next several training sessions, work on making sure that your dog honors your "leave it" training requests when you spontaneously ask her to do so from farther away and in all kinds of scenarios, such as while you're sitting on the ground or while you're opening and closing cabinets. This is harder than it sounds, so start slowly! It's like you are saying, "I want you to leave everything I've placed on the counter or table alone no matter what I'm doing when I ask you to do it." This attention to detail gets your dog rock solid on this skill.

10. Next your goal is to make the context of "leave it" even more challenging. The best teachers really get creative with this and practice this constantly in early training. Go as far as putting actual people food on a plate, set it on the ground, and request a "leave it/look at me." You are doing two things with exercises like this. You are making it clear to your dog that no matter how accessible or tempting something is, she is to leave it alone (unless given permission to eat it, of course!). If your dog leaves a real plate of food alone while on the ground during a training session like this, then she is much more likely to understand

this concept when you leave a plate of food on the table and walk away. Years ago, I used to appear on the local morning news pretty regularly to promote my dog training classes and to show off my dogs' exciting tricks and stunts. However, nothing seemed to get the audience to say, "Wow!" like my setting down a plate of fried chicken on the ground and getting my dogs to leave it alone. This is a lofty accomplishment for a dog, but it really only takes a few weeks of consistent training and follow-through. Trust me, it's nowhere near as difficult as you might expect!

11. Once you are certain that your dog is going to leave various things alone no matter what you're doing in the room and no matter how close she is to the object, gradually start walking out of the room for a brief moment or two. Don't push it! Work up to having your dog leave lots of different things alone while you step out of the room for, say, ten to thirty seconds at a time. Reward generously when she does. This may prove to be too much at first, so if your dog doesn't pass the test, polish up your easier "leave it" training drills with you in person and then try leaving the room for a second or two.

12. Ideally, you should be practicing these set-up "leave it" training sessions at home, on walks, at the park, at your friends' houses, or anywhere you take your dog. If you want your dog broadly generalizing this concept, these steps are necessary. What do you do if you notice at any time that your dog is stealing something even while supervised in a controlled setting outside of these primary lessons? Burst into a secondary training session as needed! Just as with your primary lessons, you do this by blocking access to the item, redirecting your dog's attention to you, and rewarding her for compliance.

13. What if your dog has already devoured an object you left within her reach? First, remember you should never yell at your dog— she won't have any idea why you're angry. Plus, her slipup is a reflection of a lapse in *your* training. It's not her fault. Instead, just take a step back in your training (or several steps back) and

work on all the drills I've gone over in this chapter. Of course, if you think your dog has ingested something that might harm her, call your vet.

While this may seem like a lot of work, the payoffs are huge. By being relentlessly consistent, you teach your dog to generalize that she should leave everything alone unless given permission to engage it. If you do all of this impulse control training, it makes handling unwanted behaviors such as pulling on the leash and jumping way easier. See, you are not just teaching your dog to stop stealing. You are also teaching her how to override her most basic instincts, and that is extremely powerful. These are the things that give your dog a solid foundation of knowledge to build on, especially when working around distractions in all aspects of training.

CHAPTER 12

DIGGING

Digging is a natural behavior for dogs, a way for them to inspect and explore things they're interested in. Unfortunately, they aren't born knowing that we'd prefer that they not do it—especially when they leave lots of little craters in our yards! This chapter helps you determine why your dog might dig and how to put a stop to the behavior.

WHY DO DOGS DIG?

There are two main reasons dogs dig: they're puppies or they're bored. It's common for puppies to scratch and dig at surfaces as they are just learning how to interact with everything they can in their environment. So, they'll try to use their paws as little hands. Eventually, most dogs discover that using their mouths is a more practical way to pick things up, especially if you've been showing your dog how to properly use his mouth along the way through games like tug-of-war. Even then, a dog might still use his paws from time to time.

For older dogs, digging most often occurs because they have nothing else to do. In other words, if dogs don't get enough exercise, they might spend their pent-up energy digging their yards. Dogs may also dig because they are hot and want to reveal cooler ground or because they want protection from the cold, wind, rain, and other elements.[1] They may also dig in order to attempt to break out of a contained environment, like a fenced-in yard, or because they are anxious.

Keep in mind that some digging behavior is natural and should even be allowed to an extent. For example, if a scent catches a dog's attention, he might lightly dig to further investigate where the smell is coming from. Often this type of digging is relatively shallow in depth compared to more extreme digging. However, you can still help cut back on this kind of behavior if it ever gets out of control (say, your dog wants to stop every few feet and dig every time he's out on a walk). Keep reading!

WHAT TO DO ABOUT DIGGING

Handling digging is actually pretty straightforward. In fact, I've found that making sure a dog gets regular, vigorous exercise early in the day along with controlling your dog's environment are the two keys to dramatically reducing or stopping this habit. If your dog is digging because he is fearful or anxious for some reason, then see chapters 15 and 16 on handling those issues. Of course, if your dog is digging to find a cool, warm, or dry spot, then bring him inside. Here's what else you need to know to deal with digging:

1. Dealing with "puppy digging" is very similar to resolving other unwanted behaviors. Remember that you must directly supervise your puppy when outside for a variety of reasons, not the least of which is digging. If your puppy starts to dig or seems like he might start digging—say, he begins smelling his favorite digging spot—redirect his attention first to you and then to an acceptable item, like a toy that he can play with. This may be

tough at first as sometimes the scent and texture of the ground can be very interesting. However, you want your dog engaging with you instead of the ground, so using the toy, show him how much fun tug and fetch can be.

2. If your dog is uninterested in playing with you, using a great treat to first distract him can help. Use that treat as a bridge to pay attention to you. If need be, place the treat right at his nose, touching his nose if necessary. Next, bring that treat to your eyes to encourage a "look at me." You can say, "Look at me" to get his attention. This is just a variation of the "leave it/look at me" combo. In this case, your dog is leaving the ground alone and looking at you instead. (I told you this was a handy skill!) You may need to do this for a few days or even weeks until you curb your dog's digging habit.

3. For older dogs, you need to proactively make sure your dog doesn't have the opportunity to dig. Let's say your dog is digging moderate-sized holes in your backyard when you let him run around outside. Since the first step is actually taking a step back and regaining control of the environment, have your dog on a twenty-foot leash instead. This allows him to continue to roam, sniff, and explore, but you're in total control of the situation as you've made it impossible for sustained digging to occur.

4. You know your dog and, as with puppies, you can likely detect when he is about to start digging. Again, when you sense that's the case, get your dog's attention on you with a treat or by playing as if to say, "Don't do that. Do this instead. Trust me, it's way more fun!" By interrupting the digging and replacing it with something that makes your dog happy, you'll be well on your way to getting digging under control. Whenever you are trying to get your dog to be playful with you, remember to be extra-energetic and always genuine. Also, use a high-pitched voice—research out of the University of York found that using such a tone when talking directly to a dog is the best way to get a dog's attention.[2]

5. If your dog is uninterested in playing and having treats during these moments (because he finds the ground *that* enticing), just escort him away from the immediate area and go to a different part of the yard. Try to reengage him there. If he's still uninterested in playtime or treats, then this is a sign that you need to do much more work on desensitizing him to this type of environment. In other words, you have not yet built enough communication in these types of environments to stop this behavior long term. You can fix this by spending tons of time doing basic training with him or even playing fetch with him outdoors.

Over time, your dog will get the picture that you'll interrupt his digging every time, and he'll eventually cut back or even stop the behavior. But relying on interrupting exclusively is no way to resolve this. Rather, exercise and controlling the environment is critical. Like I said before, when you address those two things, the digging will almost certainly stop.

CHAPTER 13

EATING POOP

This definitely is the grossest of all the possible behavioral issues that dogs might have. I mean, seriously—they've got their food and they've got their treats. Why in the world would they ever want to eat something as disgusting as their own poop or the poop of another animal? Well, this issue—scientifically known as *coprophagia*—is a lot more common than you might think, especially among young dogs. In this chapter, I'll help you bring this nasty habit to a stop.

WHY DO DOGS EAT POOP?

There are lots of reasons why dogs might eat their own feces or another animal's feces, ranging from having a diet deficient in certain nutrients or calories, malabsorption syndromes, various illnesses such as thyroid disease, and intestinal parasites.[1] Also, some experts say that puppies might learn the behavior from their mothers, who sometimes eat their offspring's stool to keep the den clean.[2]

A study in *Veterinary Medicine and Science* points to another possible reason: researchers surveyed more than three thousand people with dogs and discovered that of the 16 percent of dogs who ate feces often, 80 percent preferred poop that was fresh (less than two days old).[3] Coprophagia had nothing to do with the dog's breed, gender, age, or even how well they were housetrained. Instead, the study authors hypothesized that the reason stems back to dogs' wolf ancestors. Wolves would defecate away from their dens to protect against intestinal parasite eggs in the feces. However, if a sick or injured wolf did defecate near the den, they would eat the feces right away since parasite eggs don't usually hatch into infectious larvae for a few days. In other words, wolves would eat the poop to keep their den free of dangerous parasites—and the idea is that dogs today are doing the same because it's a natural instinct.

WHAT TO DO ABOUT EATING POOP

Regardless of why your dog is eating poop, getting her to stop this habit requires you to be very persistent. As with most things related to training dogs, you won't get results if you're passive about this issue. Here's what you should do instead:

1. First, check with your vet to rule out any medical reason why your dog might be eating stool.

2. Controlling your dog's environment is critical. While you're working on this issue, your dog can't just wander in the yard unattended. She should be on leash when outside so you can monitor her every move. It's also very important to be meticulous about cleaning up after her. Obviously, if your dog doesn't have access to her feces on the ground, then it's impossible for her to eat it.

3. Give your dog a treat right after she poops. That way, you direct her attention back to you *and* to something appropriate to eat! Of course, giving your dog a reward after doing her business outside has an extra benefit: it helps with potty training and

further ingrains the idea that outside (not on your carpet!) is the right place to go.

4. What if you catch your dog about to sneak herself a not-so-tasty snack? If you've really prioritized teaching and enforcing "leave it/look at me" as I explain on page 49, chapter 3, then this is just another variation. In other words, when your dog begins to indicate that she is taking an interest in poop on the ground, you'll need to promptly interrupt her and then get her attention on you by saying, "Leave it" and then "Look at me." Acknowledge her good behavior by rewarding her with a treat. Continue doing this over the course of several months, rewarding intermittently (which I describe how to do on page 195, chapter 22). However, don't let your guard down too early on this one because it takes significant time to break any behavior that has become a habit. I realize that what I just described is actually a secondary training session—you are training in a real-life moment. With most training, I'd recommend that you do primary training sessions and surprise primary training sessions first. However, that's difficult when it comes to a dog eating poop. Unlike other "leave it" training sessions that require you to practice with actual items that your dog might be interested in, that's not very practical here for obvious reasons (unless you want to start roaming your neighborhood in the off chance of finding another dog's poop that wasn't picked up). That's why it's vital to teach your dog a reliable, generalized "leave it" with many dozens of items. You want your dog to be rock solid on this no matter *what* you're asking her to leave alone.

5. As you continue working on this issue, you'll notice that you might be able to interrupt your dog's focus on poop even when she is at a distance in your yard. For example, you could supervise from your back deck while your dog takes a potty break because when you say, "Leave it," she does. But other dogs may disregard your request. In those cases, you'll need to continue having your dog on leash until she progresses further.

6. Dogs who eat poop don't necessarily discriminate on the type of poop they consume. So, what should you do if you have a cat, and your dog is eating poop out of his litterbox? Use the same logic—make sure your dog doesn't have access to the litterbox by putting it in an area only your cat can access. By managing your dog's environment and rewarding good behavior often, you'll have this taken care of in no time! As your dog gets out of the habit of eating poop, then she's less likely to continue to want it. Good luck!

CHAPTER 14

HUMPING

Humping is a natural dog behavior. When a dog humps people or objects, it's actually a very similar behavior to jumping, so you might notice some similarities in how I suggest handling it. When a dog humps other dogs, that's a little different. I'll cover both types of humping in this chapter.

WHY DO DOGS HUMP PEOPLE AND OBJECTS?

As with jumping, when dogs hump people or objects, it most often seems to occur when a dog is feeling playful or excited. Of course, regardless of the reason, humping can be pretty obnoxious, and you'll want to discourage the behavior ideally before it even starts. However, it's never too late to resolve this.

WHAT TO DO ABOUT HUMPING PEOPLE AND OBJECTS

From a training perspective, resolving humping is virtually identical to resolving jumping. Just know that this behavior quickly becomes a bad habit if it goes on too long, so work on stopping it sooner rather than later. Here's how:

1. First, see your vet to make sure the humping isn't due to a medical issue such as skin allergies, urinary incontinence, or a urinary tract infection.[1] Also, you can ask your vet whether neutering or spaying might help reduce your dog's behavior.

2. As with most unwanted energetic behaviors, exercise is key! If your dog is getting plenty of healthy play, then he won't be as excited when, say, guests come over. In turn, he'll be less likely to hump them.

3. Showing your dog the proper way to behave is critical. In this case, a sit and a stay should be the alternative behavior that you encourage. Also, humping behavior becomes pretty easy to anticipate as you get to know your dog. Therefore, being preemptive and asking for a sit and a stay any time you or others greet your dog teaches him the acceptable way to behave. Set up primary training sessions to handle this, similar to the ones I covered on jumping in chapter 6. For instance, you might have a friend or family member come over to your house so you can work on this specific issue.

4. If at any time your dog begins humping, simply redirect him by using a treat to lure him away from the person or object he's humping. Then, ask for a sit and a stay. Always have your dog's currency nearby—say, by the front door or wherever he is likely to hump—so that you are in a good position to reinforce the proper behavior. At first acknowledge subtle, brief success— say your dog sits and stays for a few seconds—and increase the duration as your dog starts reliably sitting and staying rather than humping.

WHY DO DOGS HUMP OTHER DOGS?

When dogs hump one another, it can mean a variety of things. For instance, humping can be sexual in nature, particularly for dogs who haven't been spayed or neutered. However, both male and female dogs hump, as do dogs who have been fixed.[2] Humping can certainly be a normal part of playing, too. For example, many younger dogs, especially those who haven't been properly socialized, attempt to hump other dogs in social settings. It seems to be their way of gaining control over another dog—not in an aggressive way, but apparently as a way to say, "Stay here! I want to interact with you!"

WHAT TO DO ABOUT HUMPING OTHER DOGS

Keep in mind that humping isn't always a bad thing. Context matters! If the dogs involved are behaving appropriately and seem to be tolerant of the humping, it may be fine. However, sometimes you'll want to stop the behavior. Here's how:

1. Again, first talk to your vet to make sure your dog's humping isn't due to a medical condition.

2. You might get some help from the other dogs themselves: many older, well-adapted dogs are quite good at letting younger dogs know that they need to back off. This may mean a quick harmless air snap or loud squeal. Often a few of these experiences is all it takes for dogs to learn not to hump other dogs.

3. Of course, there might be cases where you need to intervene. If you notice your dog is humping another dog and that dog seems unhappy about it, simply remove your dog from the situation and give him a brief time-out. Ask him to sit and give him a really tasty treat when he does. Once your dog seems to have chilled out a bit, let him resume playing. If he tries to hump again, give him another time-out, and consider making this one a bit longer.

By redirecting your dog every time he begins to hump, he learns that humping isn't a preferred behavior.

4. If your dog's humping is way out of hand and he seems to hump every dog that comes across his path, then you'll want to make sure he gets very vigorous exercise just before interactions with other dogs. Of course, if your dog has a bite history with other dogs, then you shouldn't let him have easy access to other dogs he doesn't know and get along with. Provided you are very consistent about bringing a prompt end to humping just before or as it begins, most dogs learn that this behavior brings an end to the fun—and they stop doing it.

CHAPTER 15

FEARS AND PHOBIAS

We've all met dogs who are total social butterflies. You know the type of dog I'm talking about: ones who always seem eager to jump in the car, explore new places, and become best friends with new people or other dogs. However, there are plenty of other dogs who instead become anxious and fearful around new people, animals, and even certain places and situations. Maybe your dog is afraid of a particular person. Maybe she thinks vacuum cleaners are the scariest things ever! Maybe the sound of the garbage truck coming down the street sends her into a total panic. Trust me, I've seen it all!

I often encounter fearful behavior with dogs I meet at my studio where I film my YouTube series. We have a thorough casting process, and I like to meet each dog and get to know them a little bit in order to find the video topic they'd be perfect for. However, not all dogs are immediately at ease in a new place. When I cast a dog for a particular lesson, I have to see how she reacts in my specific setting. For example, do the tall, top-heavy studio lights throw her off? Or can she not stand the idea of walking on wood floors? Or do new places in general cause her to act uncharacteristically? Or is she a little wary of me, a total stranger? I always make sure every dog is comfortable in the shooting environment.

If a dog is not, that's okay. I just shift gears. So, while I may intend to cast a dog for a basic lesson on fetch, if it turns out that she is too nervous to be in a playful mood, then I'll instead make the video about the more interesting topic for that dog—getting her comfortable with strangers or in a new environment.

In this chapter, we'll shed some light on why dogs are sometimes fearful and what to do to help put them at ease. First, it's important to understand the difference between fear and phobias. Whereas *fear* is a survival mechanism and a normal, proportionate response to a particular threat or circumstance, a *phobia* is an excessive, persistent fear of a stimulus out of proportion to the threat it poses, explains Stephanie Borns-Weil, DVM, DACVB, an animal behaviorist and clinical instructor at the Cummings School of Veterinary Medicine at Tufts University.[1]

Naturally, the degree of fear varies from dog to dog. In some cases, a dog might quickly learn to no longer fear the things she was previously scared of. In more extreme cases, progress may be slow and improvement—not total success—may be the ultimate end goal. Most dogs fall somewhere in between, meaning that their fear or phobia may not be eliminated but improved to varying degrees. It's always important to remember that it's not fair to insist that our dogs just accept everything and everyone in their lives, just as it wouldn't be fair to expect that of humans. Some people love skydiving, while others wouldn't do it for a million dollars (myself included!). Well, for dogs, that vacuum cleaner, thunderstorm, or dog down the street who is ten times your dog's size might very well be the equivalent from her perspective.

Of course, this is one of those topics that you need to tackle on a case-by-case basis. I'll walk you through the *basics* of what to do in each situation. But if your dog is so fearful that it affects her day-to-day life—or yours for that matter—talk to your vet and possibly an animal behaviorist in your area.

WHY DO DOGS BECOME FEARFUL?

Basically, there are a few reasons why dogs are fearful. First, just as some people are predisposed to be shyer or more scared than others, the same is true for our pets: some dogs are fearful because of genetics. They were born that way. In many other cases, a dog is afraid of something either because she has had a negative experience with it in the past or because she wasn't properly exposed to it during the critical socialization period (which is typically between six and fourteen weeks). See page 42, chapter 2, for more on the importance of socialization.

WHAT TO DO ABOUT A FEARFUL DOG

While I go over specific situations throughout the rest of this chapter, there are some essentials to dealing with a fearful dog no matter what she's afraid of specifically. Here are the most important ones:

1. First and foremost, it's essential that you have a strong bond with your dog. That is particularly true if she's apprehensive. Your dog needs to trust you as you work through these sensitive issues together. See page 7, chapter 1, for more on bonding with your dog.

2. Exercise helps tremendously with fears and phobias. I'm not saying it's a cure-all with these issues as they often run deep and require committed attention and extra training, but it can go very far in making your dog's uneasiness more manageable. This is especially true when exercise immediately precedes training—you're more likely to be successful during sessions aimed at reducing your dog's fear if she's gotten some of her energy out first. So, a workout aimed at getting your dog panting a bit is a good idea before you tackle the training sessions I've outlined in this chapter. Of course, there are some dogs who are very low-energy and not likely to want to play fetch or go on a long walk. With these dogs, go straight into training.

3. When dealing with your dog's fears, work on managing the situation so that she's not exposed to the triggers for too long or at a distance or degree that's too overwhelming for her. Instead, gradually desensitize her to those triggers and then work on counterconditioning. Also, let her choose the distance at which she's most comfortable—so, if she's afraid of, say, a particular person or object, don't make her get close to that person or object. Yes, you can work on decreasing that distance over time, but you've got to do so at your dog's pace.

4. Another part of managing the situation is timing: don't wait to do this training when you really have to go to the place or encounter the person, animal, or object that your dog is scared of. Instead,

practice in dedicated, primary training sessions so that you can completely focus on your dog.

5. Never punish your dog for being fearful. In fact, that's the absolute worst thing you can do as it can make your dog even more afraid. Instead, if you remain understanding, calm, and patient, you are likely to make strong progress.

HANDLING A FEAR OF PLACES

To handle your dog's fear, you need to attempt to change her emotional response to things that make her nervous or uneasy. Let's say your dog is afraid of certain places or new places. Here's what you can do:

1. The more a dog is in a place without something "bad" happening, the more likely she is to become accepting of that place. So, say your dog is fearful of your friend's house for one reason or another. In this case, your job is to get your dog used to going to your friend's house often so that she might become more at ease. This is desensitization.

2. It's critical that you let your dog take in new environments on her own terms. This might mean that instead of going straight to your friend's house (or whichever place makes your dog nervous), you might get her as close to the environment as you can without pushing her over her limit. So, in the case of your friend's house, you might spend some time outside of the house. Or if your dog is frightened of congested sidewalks in a crowded city, you'll need to find a place off the beaten path near those sidewalks to simply hang out and walk. For instance, sit at a café on a side street where your dog can see, hear, and smell everything happening on those congested sidewalks without being in the thick of things. The goal here is to slowly ease your dog into seeing people walk by and hearing the sounds of the city and realizing that the worst doesn't happen.

3. Focus on normalizing the place in question by getting your dog to do some light play and general training at her *working distance* (the closest she can get to the thing that causes fear while she can still pay attention). Your intention is to bring some normalcy to her world. Since you've focused on training in other environments, this is just another environment, albeit a little tougher for your dog. You are taking advantage of the fact that she has good associations with these basic training drills in other places, and you are trying to get her to make those same associations in *this* place. At first, your dog's fear may be too great to insist on too much training, but test her often to see how receptive she is to taking general direction from you. Nowhere is *tiny progress* more important than when addressing issues of anxiety or fear. Ask for a "sit," "down," or "look at me" to measure how willing your dog is to focus on normal requests. If you find that she is unresponsive to these skills when she is otherwise quickly willing to conform, this is a sign that your dog's discomfort may be too great at this point in time. Continue focusing on letting her simply exist in the closest proximity you can while she's still calm and relaxed.

4. Sometimes desensitization is enough to achieve the progress you're seeking. However, for most dogs who are fearful, counterconditioning—changing an existing undesired perception to a desired one—is also appropriate. Bring top-notch treats that your dog loves and give them to her often just to reinforce that the place is totally fun and awesome! You want her to go from thinking, "This place is scary!" to "I get to show off my skills in this place *and* get some chicken. This place is awesome."

HANDLING A FEAR OF THE GROOMER AND VET

Lots of dogs are specifically nervous at the groomer or the vet. And who can blame them? They're often held still on a cold table while a stranger pokes and prods them. I certainly wouldn't want to visit those places either!

Of course, such visits are often necessary, but how do you make your dog less afraid of these places? The key is to make sure that you spend time at those places outside of normally scheduled visits. Don't wait until you actually have a vet or groomer appointment to teach your dog to overcome any anxious feelings. Instead, talk to your vet or groomer about bringing your dog to the office or salon several times a month when you don't have an appointment. Once there, give your dog time to adjust—which can take twenty minutes or longer. Just be low key and let her chill out at the vet or groomer without anything bad happening. By experiencing these places often, your dog is more likely to generalize them as "normal."

Also, do some counterconditioning with basic training by giving her treats to communicate that this environment can mean getting things you really like! You might even ask the vet, groomer, and other staff members to ask your dog to sit and then give her treats. In other words, you want your dog thinking that the vet or groomer is a normal, fun environment—not a totally scary place.

What about when you have to go to these places for a real appointment? First, exercise your dog before the visit to help reduce her anxiety. Also, explain to, say, your vet that your dog is fearful and that you might need some help getting her to relax a little bit. Bring treats and encourage your vet and anyone who works at the office to reward your dog for any positive interaction. For example, as your dog steps on the scale and simply stays there for a moment, they can give her a reward. As they touch your dog for a moment, they can give her a reward. With very small steps like this, you are more likely to get your dog to accept the vet's office. See my video *How to Train Your Puppy to Love the Vet!* for a vivid illustration of how to do this.

CAN DOGS HAVE OCD?

Some dogs exhibit compulsive behaviors such as pacing, circling, tail chasing, fly biting, and nonstop barking. Others chase objects that aren't there or they lick certain parts of their bodies incessantly. So what are these behaviors all about? They are actually very similar to OCD in humans. "Dogs with OCD exhibit behaviors out of context and/or excessive to their actual need to accomplish the apparent goal," explains Karen L. Overall, VMD, PhD, a leading veterinary behaviorist, senior research scientist at the University of Pennsylvania, and founding researcher of the Canine Behavioral Genetics Project.[3] "For instance, most dogs who clean their fur don't lick to the bone, but those with OCD might. A dog might chase a fly and stop whenever the fly leaves, but one with OCD will obsessively chase flies even if none are there. Once these behaviors are established, they are also out of context in terms of degree, frequency, form, and intensity. They also interfere with the dog's ability to respond normally to social stimuli and even to pain."

If you think your dog might be exhibiting OCD behaviors, first talk to your vet to rule out a medical illness and to determine the best course of action, such as medication. However, it's critical to understand the cause of OCD behaviors. "The physical manifestations—the tail chasing, the licking, the sucking—are the result of an underlying profound anxiety," says Dr. Overall. "I have never been able to treat a dog for OCD without treating their anxiety."

In other words, use this chapter to help your dog cope with anything that is making her particularly nervous or afraid. Again, this will be a mix of managing your dog's environment, desensitizing her to the triggers, and counterconditioning. Of course, always make sure your dog is getting plenty of exercise. "Dogs with OCD might be particularly primed to enjoy rule-based activities such as flyball and agility courses since these activities give them a format for structured and repeated activity," says Dr. Overall. "However, remember such activities will not treat OCD alone, and if a dog's OCD worsens after doing them, stop."

Remember, you have to work with your vet and possibly an animal behaviorist to get a proper diagnosis. "We have to be careful that we do not medicalize normal behaviors," says Dr. Overall. "For instance, some active dogs pace a lot because they are not getting enough exercise." In other words, don't immediately assume your dog has OCD because, chances are, she just has a little extra energy to burn.

HANDLING A FEAR OF CAR RIDES

Lots of dogs get really anxious about car rides. It must seem pretty odd to them, right? They get into this object and it moves and turns erratically, while the floor beneath them bumps and vibrates. Also, some dogs experience car sickness, just as humans do. First, for dogs younger than one year old, the parts of the inner ear involved with balance might not yet be fully developed.[4] Also, stress can make a dog queasy—maybe your dog has had bad experiences in the car so far and when faced with having to take another ride, she becomes anxious.

So, what do you do? Well, if your dog is getting carsick, make sure you don't feed her right before a car ride. Also, talk to your vet about medication that might help. Other than that, it's important to get your dog comfortable with car rides so she's no longer afraid of them. This is a perfect example of how desensitization works! Many dogs just need time to adjust to cars, and the more experience your dog has in them, the more normal they will seem.

At first, you might need to start *really* slowly and do some counter-conditioning using a parked car in your driveway. Maybe your first step is simply to get your dog within five feet of the car. That's fine! Give her a treat for being so brave. Work up to having her sniff the car. Again, reward accordingly! Or maybe you're at the point where you have your dog stick her head in the car to investigate. Give her a treat to pair that experience with something great. Some dogs start accepting the car in a single training session. Others take weeks.

You can manage your dog's fear and anxiety related to cars by keeping training rides short. For example, you can drive around the block just to give her some exposure. Several trips that last just a few minutes might help ease your dog into the process of being in a car. It might even be a good idea to have someone in the backseat offer your dog some yummy treats while you take these rides. Often, though, with car rides, you have a great opportunity to provide a great outcome with the destination itself. For years, I'd drive all of my dogs to the park often, which they loved because they knew they'd get to play Frisbee there. Over time, they learned to generalize the car as a pretty cool thing—they'd enthusiastically jump in the car with their tails wagging any time I asked.

Sure, I'd take them for their vet and grooming appointments, but they didn't only associate the car with unpleasant things. Once your dog begins to anticipate the destination as being a fun place, she'll likely become more accepting of the car. On the flip side, if you really only drive your dog when it's time for a vet or grooming appointment, you might find car rides with her a continuous struggle.

HANDLING NOISE PHOBIAS

Noise phobias are very common among dogs. How are they supposed to understand that fireworks, construction sounds, the noise of the garbage truck, or thunder are harmless? They certainly don't sound harmless! Also, as I mentioned on page 57, chapter 4, dogs have much more sensitive hearing than humans do, so while, say, the sound of the smoke detector going off or a police siren might not seem scary to you, it sounds like the end of the world to your dog.[5] You've got to go out of your way to create positive associations with these things—the earlier and more often, the better!

I've dealt with *a lot* of dogs who are very afraid of particular noises. For instance, I recently worked with Riker, an adorable rescue dog. I was meeting him for the first time to see what kind of video I could do with him. Everything started off quite well. He was eager to play with me and was very responsive to training.

However, his family told me that they lived near train tracks and this sweet, lovable dog's demeanor would totally change whenever a train went by. His anxiety levels would just skyrocket. He'd whimper, hide, and take a very long time to calm down even after the train passed. Often dogs like this tend to get nervous around a variety of sounds, so I decided to take the training session outside in the yard. Sure enough, we were playing fetch together when Riker suddenly froze and seemed to completely lose interest in anything I was doing. Instead, he retreated to the back door of the house. He wouldn't budge. It took me a moment to figure out what was going on. There was no train. However, a few houses down, a new roof was being installed and the sound of the construction appeared to be the culprit.

This called for one of those unplanned secondary training sessions to address Riker's fear, so I pulled out some treats and began giving him small pieces in the presence of this noise. I stayed with him at the back door, and I didn't force him to come onto the lawn. In other words, I wanted to work where *he* was most comfortable outside. The construction was several houses away, so the noise was faint. However, had the house been directly next door, it would have been more ideal to go inside and do the same lesson as the sound would have been *too* daunting for him. Meanwhile, Riker ended up doing great. His fear did eventually pass, and we were able to continue playing and training. The video is titled *How to Reassure Dogs When Something Throws Them Off.*

Of course, you'd have to continue sessions like this for at least several months to see longer-lasting results, but what a great start! The process of just giving Riker treats that he liked while in the presence of a noise he didn't like communicated, "See! That noise isn't all bad! Good things happen when you hear that noise. You're safe, you get good treats, and the world doesn't end!" Here are some more specifics on how to handle two very common noise phobias: thunderstorms and fireworks.

Thunderstorm Phobia

From a training perspective, one of the problematic aspects to addressing a phobia of thunderstorms is that it's difficult to set up training sessions. Sure, it's not impossible. I guess you could anticipate many thunderstorms by checking the weather and keeping an eye on the Doppler radar. However, working through noise phobias often requires a heavy emphasis on unplanned secondary training sessions, too.

So, when you hear that first rumble of thunder, grab some chicken from the fridge and rapidly toss tiny pieces to your dog. Once again, you are trying to reverse the perception of, "Thunder is so scary" to "Thunder means I get a lot of chicken!" Assuming your dog takes the treats, do some light, easy training to keep your dog's mind off of things. I have found that by doing normal activities that dogs are used to during moments like this, they might be less focused on things that throw them off.

Of course, if your dog has a well-established fear of thunder, then progress is likely to be *very* slow at first. She may not want treats at all. Trust me, I get it! My dog Venus was so terrified of thunderstorms that even chicken wasn't enough to get her mind off of roaring thunder. So, what should you do in such cases? This is why desensitizing a dog is the other part of the equation. While counterconditioning with treats works with some dogs, for others you really need to make her calm around the noise *first*. For example, while Venus wasn't much of a cuddler, she would be the best cuddler in the world if she heard thunder. Sometimes, cuddling seemed to reduce her anxiety the most. She'd hop up on the couch and press up against me, and I'd reassure her and pet her softly. I would keep my demeanor calm and neutral because I knew if I acted as though things were normal, she might take that as a cue to relax a bit. *My goal was to reduce her anxiety in the presence of thunder for even just a few minutes.* The more minutes you get of that minimized fear, the more likely your dog's behavior is to improve over time. If lying next to me on the couch helped, then this was a step in the right direction. Other times during storms, Venus loved to nestle in the bathroom or bedroom closet. She seemed to feel safer there. And since she would appear more relaxed and less stressed, I considered that very valuable desensitization time as well.

In other words, when dealing with your dog's fear, it's so important to meet her in the middle. So, while I would have preferred that Venus just take the bits of chicken and cooperate on staying focused on training or playing, I also understood that if she felt safer next to me or in the closet, I could accept that as progress, too. I wouldn't say that Venus ever came to enjoy thunderstorms, but she did exhibit dramatic progress over the years.

Fireworks Phobia

You should handle fireworks in a similar way to thunderstorms. When you hear that first round of firecrackers going off in the late afternoon on the Fourth of July or on New Year's Eve, schedule in some training time to desensitize and countercondition your dog. Teach your dog that fireworks equal something awesome like treats or play! If you can actually get your dog taking treats or playing with you in the presence of these nerve-wracking sounds, you are well on your way to progress.

My youngest dog, Alpha Centauri, was anxious about fireworks. I remember one Fourth of July, there were fireworks all over the place and my wife, Bree, and I were enjoying them. However, I get that, to a dog, it probably felt like our neighborhood was under siege by an occupying force! Alpha Centauri, being the ball-obsessed dog that he was, sat there looking at his ball while flinching at every pop and bang. He desperately wanted to play (as usual!) but was having a hard time tuning out distractions as he normally did flawlessly. I wanted to help him through this issue, so I tossed the ball a few feet into the yard and he pursued it, albeit a bit more reluctantly. The fireworks were in full bloom, and he was awkwardly trying to keep track of the ball while contending with those fireworks. It was a full-on war zone! However, after a few more tosses, he eventually tuned out those fireworks. It was so gratifying to see that! After this incident, Bree and I nicknamed him "Battledog." Over the years, Alpha Centauri's anxiety about fireworks diminished greatly. I just always made sure I had a ball ready to toss to him on days when I knew there would be fireworks in our neighborhood, like New Year's Eve and the Fourth of July.

The point of this story is that in the case of any loud noise, try to find something your dog *loves* and get her doing that instead! It might be fetch, it might be easy training sessions, or it might be simply giving her amazing treats. Just go out of your way to create desirable outcomes to things that might not be so fun for your dog. Don't wait until her fear is in full bloom to then address it. Instead, you've got to be one step ahead of your dog's fear if you hope to make progress.

HANDLING A FEAR OF OTHER DOGS AND PEOPLE

In many cases, when dogs are fearful around people or other dogs, it might seem that socialization wasn't prioritized when they were young. Then again, there are some dogs who are just not very happy around other animals or people even when you do socialize them. Dogs can be just as reserved and introverted as people can be! In fact, many of the dogs I've met over the years were very reserved—they were content to just be around their people but couldn't care less about being around other people and dogs. Or maybe you did socialize your dog, but she had a series of bad experiences that caused her to regress and become afraid in certain situations.

Regardless of why your dog might be afraid of people and other dogs, it's critical that you work on this issue. That's because your dog is very likely to encounter other people and other dogs in her life, so teaching her to react appropriately is vital—especially since fear can lead to aggressive behaviors. While some dogs may cower and roll onto their backs when approached by another dog or a stranger, others might snap or bite if suddenly approached. Therefore, you'll need to manage your dog's access to other dogs and people while you work through her fears. (See chapter 18 on aggression to learn ways you can prevent your dog from harming others.)

It's worth reemphasizing that the more deep-rooted a fear is, the longer it might take to see dramatic improvement—I'm talking months or longer. And in extreme cases, you might never eliminate the fear altogether. You might have to accept progress as your success.

Fear of Other Dogs

Let's say your dog is scared of other dogs. Here's what you can do:

1. Your first objective is simply to get your dog comfortable and content in the presence of dogs at a distance. This is the desensitization phase. You're teaching your dog that it's "normal" to be around other dogs. This might mean going to a large park during off-peak hours and allowing your dog to see, smell, and hear dogs from a hundred or more yards away. Your goal is to find that distance at which your dog is comfortable being around other dogs.

2. Once you feel your dog has settled into the new environment in or even near the park, do some counterconditioning so that you might get your dog to connect "dogs in the distance" with something she perceives as enjoyable like great treats or playtime! So, ask for a "sit" and a "down." Reward generously. If she is too

thrown off by the environment, let her just exist calmly and do what you can to get her in a good mood in the way only *you* can.

3. You may have to spend months or even years working on this issue. Work up to your dog being able to get closer and closer to other dogs, but do not overwhelm her at any point. One bad incident where you push your dog too quickly can really set her back and negate a lot of the progress you already made. Also, remember that all dogs are not destined to love other dogs. And that's okay! It doesn't matter if your dog hates other dogs as long as she keeps away from them and doesn't start trouble. In other words, it's just important that your dog learns to behave appropriately when other dogs are in the vicinity. Again, until then, you must manage her responsibly in the ways we've covered in this chapter.

My own dog Venus never really loved other dogs, but she learned to tolerate them. Throughout her life, we played in countless public parks, and we had to contend with happy, goofy dogs running around off leash from time to time. Venus wanted nothing to do with them as she was always all business. That was her personality. She was there to play Frisbee for as long as she could, not to playfully engage with a new dog she just met.

Venus and I had the "agreement" that she would go into a down and a stay any time there was an off-leash dog in the vicinity, and I would keep the dog from harassing her by either standing between her and the dog or even by picking the other dog up when he or she got too close (if I felt safe doing so, of course!). I do believe that if Venus hadn't had frequent, distant access to many unfamiliar dogs throughout her life, she might not have been so tolerant of other dogs if left to her own devices. It seems that this combination of exercising and regularly being around dogs in the distance really made a difference in her case.

Fear of People

Some dogs are fearful of people. The good news is that it's easy to control and direct other people in their interactions with your dog. For example, it's simple enough to say to a visitor, "Give my dog some space, please. She's timid with strangers at first." It's also easy to set up favorable outcomes around people as you can manipulate the distance they are from your dog, which is critical to reducing your dog's anxiety. Here's what you can do:

1. If your dog is nervous about visitors, first find the ideal distance at which your dog is likely to relax. This might mean that your visitor sits on your living room couch while your dog relaxes on the other side of the room. This is a wonderful way to desensitize your dog to being around the guest.

2. The more time that passes and the less pressure you put on your dog, the more likely things are to improve. Some dogs just need a few minutes to check people out at a distance. The same goes for people in public. Go out of your way to find lots of low-key public places, like parks, where your dog can do this. As your dog becomes more comfortable, you can focus on desensitizing her at closer ranges.

3. Assuming your dog isn't likely to bite out of fear, encourage your guest or someone at the park to get low to the ground and offer their hand to be sniffed. Then give the person a great treat to give to your dog. At first, your guest may need to toss the treat from several feet away. That's fine! If your dog learns that she receives treats from strangers routinely *and* that nothing bad happens, she's likely to become much less fearful over time. If, however, your dog is too stressed out by the person, then you yourself can offer treats and request normal behaviors like "sit" and "down." Of course, reward generously in these cases.

4. If you find that your dog is particularly uneasy around people in uniform, in big hats, or any other quirky thing, apply the same advice I've covered in this chapter. In a nutshell: Do lots of meticulous counterconditioning exercises to create the association that being around such things yields great outcomes for your dog. And, as always, go slowly!

HANDLING A FEAR OF OBJECTS

If your dog is afraid of objects like vacuums, umbrellas, or anything else, you can use a simple formula to make dramatic progress. Let's take vacuums. Rather than just turning one on as normal, set up a training session. Turn the vacuum on for a fraction of a second and give your dog a treat. Do this several times in a row. Work up to one or two seconds. Reward generously if your dog remains calm.

If your dog gets too nervous, then you are probably going too fast. Slow down! It's perfectly fine for this to take several training sessions before seeing lots of progress. As your dog gets the hang of things, practice these same exercises running the vacuum for twenty or thirty seconds at a time, provided things are going well. Do you see what you're doing? First, you are managing the situation by keeping the vacuum on for only a short period of time rather than simply expecting your dog to accept it. Next, you are providing good outcomes around the vacuum by offering fantastic treats. In other words, you're counterconditioning! You're also desensitizing your dog by repeating this drill often.

Maybe your dog is scared of umbrellas. I mean they are pretty crazy, right—they go from straight and narrow to rapidly expanding in just a second. That must be wild from a dog's perspective! So, in this case, let your dog look at the umbrella and offer a treat. Do this several times in a row. Then, open up the umbrella 5 percent of the way. Reward. Work up to slowly opening up the umbrella 50 percent of the way. You get the point! Repeat this drill often until your dog becomes more accepting of umbrellas. Again, this is counterconditioning and desensitizing.

I put this formula into practice in my video *How to Get Your Dog to Listen to You Around Anything—Even Vacuum Cleaners!* In it, I work with Jacob, an awesome dog I've done a ton of videos with. Jacob is very high-energy to say the least and, at first, he was very excited around motorized objects such as vacuum cleaners. He would bark uncontrollably. However, as you can see in the video, it took only a few minutes to teach Jacob how to behave more politely around the vacuum and other motorized objects.

Just remember that any time you want to make your dog more comfortable with something, you'll need to be fair and give her the time she requires to become comfortable. By keeping her anxiety low through effective management, by frequent, low-level exposure, and by involving things your dog loves when around places, people, animals, or anything that she's afraid of, you'll be well on your way!

CHAPTER 16

SEPARATION ANXIETY

Most dogs truly enjoy being around people. After all, that's a big reason why we love them so much! So, it's no wonder that when we leave our dogs for periods of time, they may feel uneasy or stressed out. Like all forms of anxiety or fear, the spectrum is wide as to how significant separation anxiety can be from dog to dog.

Symptoms of separation anxiety often include prolonged barking and whimpering, pacing, drooling, digging, chewing, and scratching—particularly at doors and windows.[1] Your dog might try to break out of his confinement and have potty accidents even after you've adequately walked him. Also, if your dog follows you around everywhere when you are with him, he's more likely to be anxious when you are away. Never punish your dog for any of these behaviors—doing so only makes his anxiety worse!

Of course, lots of dogs might whine a little or get into some mischief when left alone if they aren't confined in a safe space and especially if they haven't been trained properly yet. That's normal. Also, if your puppy is chewing stuff up, has frequent accidents, and barks a lot when you're not near him, these aren't necessarily signs that your dog has long-term, generalized separation anxiety. Those behaviors can simply be due to the young age of your dog. Many puppies are anxious when you first bring them home simply because they are in a brand-new place.

However, according to the *Merck Veterinary Manual*, about "14 percent of dogs have separation anxiety, or an inability of the pet to find comfort when separated from family members."[2] These dogs experience real distress when their person leaves them. In this chapter, we'll explain what to do if you're dealing with this issue.

WHY DO DOGS EXPERIENCE SEPARATION ANXIETY?

Often, separation anxiety occurs when a dog is very bored and understimulated. We underestimate just how much extra training and exercise some dogs really need to be fulfilled. Also, a change in a dog's routine seems to be a cause of separation anxiety. In fact, according to the American Society for the Prevention of Cruelty to Animals, "because far more dogs who have been adopted from shelters have this behavior problem than those kept by a single family since puppyhood, it is believed that loss of an important person or group of people in a dog's life can lead to separation anxiety."[3] So, if you've adopted a dog who is anxious, that could be one reason why he's like that. Another example: If your dog suddenly seems stressed, it could be due to a change in his home life, such as when a kid leaves for college, a roommate moves out, or a couple splits up.

Separation anxiety may also be an unintended side effect of the domestication process with many dogs. Remember that humans bred dogs who worked well in partnerships with us. The dogs best at working with people also tend to be the ones who naturally love being with people. Something is often missing for these dogs: frequent mentally and physically engaging stimulation. In other words, dogs have been selectively bred to work with people, so being left alone is just not normal to them. "Dogs are social creatures who do not generally do well with lengthy solitary confinement," explains Stephanie Borns-Weil, DVM,

DACVB, an animal behaviorist and clinical instructor at the Cummings School of Veterinary Medicine at Tufts University. "It's just not natural for them to spend many hours a day alone."[4]

WHAT TO DO ABOUT SEPARATION ANXIETY

Of course, when it comes to separation anxiety, every dog is different. You'll have to tailor your approach to your dog's individual personality. However, there are some general ways to deal with this issue. First, you've got to make sure your dog gets enough exercise. In fact, you will likely find that regular exercise dramatically reduces separation anxiety provided that it is a regular part of your dog's life! A study in *PLOS One* found that daily exercise was the largest environmental factor that was significantly different between dogs with separation anxiety and dogs with no symptoms of such anxiety.[5] If your dog is mentally and physically satisfied, he's less likely to become anxious.

What's the best way to exercise your dog? I think you know where I'm going with this: teach fetch! I've said it many times in this book, but it really does work. Playing fetch early in the day and before leaving for significant periods of time will really help your dog keep calm. See page 149, chapter 17 to get a full description of how to teach fetch. If your dog isn't into fetch or he hasn't learned it yet, then make sure to take him on a long walk in proportion to his needs.

Also, it's important to understand that dogs are incredibly observant of our behaviors, and they are particularly astute at correlating our actions with being left alone for a noticeable period of time. Let's take an obvious example: when you pick up your car keys, you usually leave the house for a while. This does not go unnoticed by most dogs. In fact, if your dog suffers from separation anxiety, this is likely to trigger a reaction from him.

When you want to change a dog's emotional response to something, counterconditioning is enormously important. Also, as with almost everything in dog training, you must not wait until a real-life circumstance arises to then address the undesired behavior. Rather, you must prepare and rehearse for these events over a period of weeks to months. My YouTube video *What to Do About Your Dog's Separation Anxiety* helps a great deal with this issue. Also, here's a step-by-step guide:

1. It's important to set up counterconditioning exercises to improve the way your dog responds to common departure signs, like your picking up your keys, opening the door, putting on your jacket, grabbing your purse or wallet, and so on. When you are at home with your dog, pick up your keys as you normally might when you are about to leave. As you do so, give your dog a treat. Playtime isn't recommended here as this is likely to get your dog more rambunctious and less likely to settle down, which is the ultimate goal. Repeat this exercise many times during your first training session or two. The idea is simply to get your dog to associate picking up the keys (and other events surrounding your departure) with getting something great. If you do this over a few training sessions, you ought to notice that your dog eagerly begins anticipating a treat. This is evidence that your dog's emotional response to your picking up the keys, putting on your coat, and opening the door is gradually becoming more favorable than usual.

2. Once you've been successful here, it's time to introduce longer-lasting toys or bones that can keep your dog's interest for an extended period of time. For instance, there are products you can stuff with treats that release the treats slowly. You might also want to consider a hollowed-out bone that you can fill with peanut butter, a pig's ear, or a safe edible bone that will take a while to eat. Now set up a drill: Put on your coat and give your dog the toy or bone for a few seconds. Take it back and let your dog forget about it for a minute. Then, pick up your keys and give the amazing toy or bone back for a minute or so. Repeat this exercise often, for five minutes at a time, throughout the day. These special toys should *only* be used during these training exercises and later when you actually leave your dog alone. See what we're doing here? We are trying to change your dog's perception of, "Oh no! You're leaving! What am I going to do?" to "Oh yay, you're

leaving! I get that special toy!" You need to get your dog enjoying the stuffed bone or toy while in your presence at first, not when you actually leave the house for real. That's because your dog's level of anxiety about your departure probably outweighs his desire to enjoy even the most amazing toy (or even a T-bone steak for that matter!). As people, we can identify with this a little bit. Think about how difficult it is to enjoy things you normally love when you're feeling anxious. For example, when you are feeling especially nervous about a test or a business decision or anything going on in your life, you're probably not as into your favorite TV shows or shopping or even your favorite meals. It's the same for dogs.

3. Next, once you've done exercises like picking up your keys and other events that your dog has associated with your leaving, and you've provided alternative, desirable outcomes to these actions, try pretending to leave the house. With some dogs, the moment they see you walk out of the door, they go into panic mode. So, instead, walk out of the door for one second, return, and give your dog that special toy or bone. Sit with him for a moment. Pick up the toy or bone, place it out of his reach so he forgets about it for a moment, and repeat this exercise a few minutes later. At first, get him comfortable with the format of these training exercises. As he comes to anticipate his special toy or treat, you can then try to leave for longer periods of time—say, five minutes or so. If that's successful, gradually add more time.

4. What about when you have to leave your home for real? Ideally, get your dog used to your being away for short periods of time— say, thirty minutes, not hours. However, I understand that slowly phasing in alone time like this isn't easy for most people. I mean, you have to go to work and continue to do the things that life demands. In these cases, you may need to find ways for your dog to have some social time with other people or dogs when you're out of the house: you might want to look into doggy day care or at least have a neighbor or relative stop by your house during the day. Apps such as Rover can also help you find dogsitters in your

area. Eventually, you might be able to leave your dog for hours at a time, but I advise avoiding that while you're actively working on mitigating separation anxiety. A study in *Applied Animal Behaviour Science* found that dogs are affected by the amount of time they are left alone.[6] If you must leave your dog home alone while you're working on his separation anxiety, then definitely make sure he gets *a lot* of exercise right before you leave.

5. Keep in mind that dogs with separation anxiety do not usually do well in crates or small areas. So, when you have to leave the house, you'll need to explore ways to safely contain your dog in a larger area, such as in a laundry room or other area of the house where your dog is likely to feel comfortable.

6. For those of you with younger dogs (and puppies especially), you've probably noticed that your dog exhibits lots of signs of separation anxiety. After all, young dogs are much like toddlers in this way—they are more likely to stress out when alone. You can still apply the steps we've covered in this chapter, but avoid having dogs under a year old spend too much time alone anyway. Puppies require lots of extra attention in their first year of training. Also, if you've adopted an older dog with little training, he may well need many of the same considerations as a young puppy as it relates to separation anxiety. Many dogs need time to be prepared to be left alone, just as kids do.

Remember, separation anxiety varies greatly and, in some cases, you might notice quick improvement, particularly if you follow my advice on exercising your dog just before you have to leave the house. However, other dogs will be on the more extreme end of the spectrum. For these dogs, keep in mind that extended management may be necessary to see improvement. That might take months—or it could last a lifetime.

In other words, some dogs may never feel completely comfortable alone, so do your best to reduce your dog's anxiety over the long run by following the advice in this chapter. The good news is that most dogs *will* eventually learn to do just fine on their own, particularly as they get older and have more training under their belts.

CHAPTER 17

HYPERACTIVITY

General hyperactivity is way up there on the list of what people tell me they want to fix with their dogs. There are actually a host of additional "problems" stemming from what people consider hyperactivity: for example, usually a dog who jumps a lot, chews things up, pulls on a leash, and seems to have a hard time focusing are the ones classified as "too hyper." This chapter addresses hyperactivity in depth.

WHY ARE SOME DOGS HYPERACTIVE?

First, it's important to understand what hyperactivity really means. Actually, it's a bit confusing. Yes, those dogs who jump, chew, and pull on leash seem hyperactive, but the behaviors they are exhibiting are normal. As I've mentioned throughout this book, dogs have been undergoing refinement for thousands of years in terms of what we've selected for when breeding them. Historically, the most valuable dogs were often the ones who seemed to have eternal stamina. That energy came in handy, for example, on the farm when livestock needed herding and when hunters needed assistance for hours on end. Along with their genetic makeup, some dogs also seem hyper because of lack of socialization, lack of training, and lack of exercise.

However, there are some dogs whose hyper behavior may actually be due to a physiological disorder. Known as *hyperkinesis*,[1] this condition can be what some researchers consider a canine form of attention deficit hyperactivity disorder (ADHD).[2] "Hyperkinesis is a pathologic behavior and is characterized by a dog who is easily stimulated into activity but cannot settle down," says John Ciribassi, DVM, DACVB, past president of the American Veterinary Society of Animal Behavior and coeditor of the book *Decoding Your Dog*.[3] Such dogs might have a hard time sitting still. They can't rest, even if their surroundings are quiet, and they never get used to the stimuli in their environment.

WHAT TO DO ABOUT HYPERACTIVITY

With the help of your vet, try to determine if your dog has so much energy she doesn't know how to channel it or if she's dealing with a more serious issue. If you think your dog is truly hyperkinetic—signs include an inability to completely relax, short attention span, reactivity to routine stimuli, and increased heart and respiratory rates[4]—then work with your vet and possibly an animal behaviorist to determine which combination of behavior modification, and possibly, medication, can help.

However, for the *vast* majority of you, your dog likely won't have hyperkinesis. Instead, that "hyperactivity" is actually just the fact that your dog is bursting with energy and needs to learn to calm down a bit. I can't stress this enough! I know that a lot people assume that hyperkinesis is an explanation for their dog's excessive energy. In fact, I hear, "I think my dog has ADHD" all the time. And while that is possibly the case for some dogs, it is not for most dogs.

So, what should you do? First, see previous chapters that described how to teach your dog to avoid jumping, begging, and so on. Also, remember that it's essential to make sure you regularly exercise your dog before teaching her basic impulse control and manners.

Most importantly, your dog needs an acceptable outlet that satisfies her desire to expend all of that incredible energy! While you may not need to give her a job, like hunting or herding, you do need to provide alternative activities. However, you've got to choose wisely. Dogs, especially hyper dogs, won't adequately exercise themselves even when they have a massive yard to run around in. And while playing with other dogs is nice and there are tons of reasons to encourage this, it isn't likely to mentally satisfy a dog enough to dramatically reduce hyperactivity.

Your best bet is an activity that involves a lot of interaction from you, like fetch. It can take several weeks to a few months to teach a proper game of fetch, so in the meantime (and as a supplement to your dog's regular exercise regimen), you can take her for long walks and go for hikes. Also, consider getting involved with fun dog sports such as Frisbee, dock diving, agility, and flyball. However, I'll reiterate that playing fetch is the most efficient way to get your dog to chill out and be content as can be.

I meet a fair amount of resistance from everyday people on this point from, time to time. For example, I commonly hear statements like, "I tried teaching my dog fetch, but she doesn't bring the toy back," "She won't let go of the toy," or "She gets distracted too easily and loses interest." What many people fail to realize is that teaching a reliable game of fetch to a dog takes weeks, even months sometimes. It is a project. However, it's some of the most valuable time you can spend on training high-energy dogs like this. Imagine being able to get all of that excess energy out of your dog on your terms and schedule quickly and efficiently. In other words, fetch is *the* way to convert a crazy, hyper dog to the most well-behaved dog on Earth.

Fetch

I cover fetch in depth on YouTube—there are tons of videos to choose from, such as *Everything You Need to Know to Teach Your Dog a Perfect Fetch!*—but here's a step-by-step guide to help you along:

1. Fetch is when your dog chases a toy, instantly picks it up, returns promptly in a straight line to you, instantly lets go of the toy, and eagerly awaits the next throw. Start by teaching a solid game of

tug (including "let go"), which I fully detail on page 79, chapter 7. In these early stages, use a toy that you can easily play tug with, like a Frisbee or tug toy. Try a variety of toys to see what your dog likes. No matter what you choose, make that toy *very* exciting and intriguing by moving it around like a wiggly snake on the ground or by playing with the toy yourself. You want to help make your dog think, "Wow! This is the coolest object ever!"

2. Keep your dog on a long fifteen- to twenty-foot lead, even if your yard or the area where you are training is fenced. You must be able to gently guide your dog back to you very consistently and prevent your dog from running around erratically. And since "keep-away" is a thrilling natural game for most dogs—you know, when your dog has an object and starts running away from you so that you have no choice but to chase her—having your dog on a long lead like this eliminates that problematic, almost certain aspect of teaching fetch.

3. When teaching fetch early on, focus on the mechanics of the game, not on actually exercising your dog. Once your dog has mastered the concept of "tug vigorously and let go instantly," it's time to start tossing the toy short distances. Toss it a foot or two and, after your dog gets it, encourage her to come back by being extra-animated and excited. I'm not kidding: keep these initial throws *very* short! Your goal is for your dog to master fetch, so keep things easy for your dog at this point.

4. When your dog returns to you, genuinely and enthusiastically offer encouragement and praise. Reward her with a brief game of tug. Say something like, "Yes, *good* dog! You are amazing!" Do not insist on an immediate drop when your dog comes back to you at this point. It's more important to keep your dog enthused about the game. Instead, give her a thirty-second game of tug as if to say to her, "You brought it back! Let's have fun for a second!" Remember that tug is a very powerful currency for dogs who like this game! Use it to your advantage often. That's why I encourage people to use playtime and not food as the currency when teaching

fetch. Dogs don't usually play anywhere near as vigorously when they are in "food mode," and it's important that they are amped up and very excited to play when you're teaching fetch in these early stages. The reason you only throw the toy a foot or two here is that if your dog does not bring the toy back, you are close enough that you can still promptly start playing tug with her to keep the "fire" going and to keep her from losing interest. So think about it: if you drop the toy a foot away and you instantly start playing tug with her just after she picks it up, she begins to equate, "I pick up the toy and a tug happens a moment later!" That means you're on the right track!

5. Continue focusing on short reps that involve your tossing the toy a few feet and then getting your dog to pick it up, come back to you in a straight line, and let go when asked (while occasionally playing some extended tug to keep things exciting). Repeat this often and then, after you've been successful for many reps, gradually extend the distance that you throw the toy.

6. Keep in mind that while dogs sure do have stamina, fetch is a sprinting activity. If your dog seems to lose interest, there's a good chance she just needs a break for five minutes. So, give your dog breaks frequently. For example, say you're teaching fetch over a period of forty-five minutes. You might play two minutes of fetch and then follow that with a two-minute break. Or you might play five minutes and then have a five-minute break. This varies from dog to dog, but remember that even if you're training for forty-five minutes, your dog should only be running for about fifteen to twenty minutes total.

7. While your dog is learning fetch, significant walks should also be part of your exercise schedule if you want to help minimize hyperactivity. For example, do your fetch training early in the day. Once you're done, take a thirty-minute walk or so (more with some dogs, less with others). You should notice immediate improvement of your dog's behavior.

CHAPTER 18

AGGRESSION

The word *aggression* is a rather loaded term in the dog training world. It can mean different things to different people. As I mentioned in my first book, I define *aggression* as follows: "When a dog deliberately growls, bites, snaps, or acts in a way meant to ensure his own perceived safety or the safety of someone or something that he values."

Often, the general public uses the term *aggressive* very liberally. For example, when a dog barks enthusiastically at another dog on a walk or jumps on people without regard, he is often described as aggressive by the average person. Also, some dogs might have altercations with other dogs at some point in their lives. Those dogs, too, might be labeled aggressive. What's wrong with that? First, all dogs who exhibit aggressive behaviors are not the same. Some might simply air snap to make their point while others might attempt to actually bite another dog or human. What's more, labeling a dog as aggressive is dangerous. These are often the dogs who needlessly wind up in shelters because their families don't know how to handle them[1]—and many of these dogs are then, in turn, euthanized.[2] Remember, dogs themselves are not aggressive. Their behaviors sometimes are.

All dogs can show aggressive behaviors like growling, snapping, teeth baring, or even biting if provoked. For instance, my coauthor's dog, Brody, is the sweetest, most affectionate pet she's ever had. But if you try to grab his favorite bone out of his mouth, he growls and might even snap at the air. Does that make him a violent, dangerous dog? No! It's just his way of saying, "Hey, this is my toy. Don't touch it." I'm not saying this behavior is ideal, but it's a far cry from a dog who seems to always be ready for a fight. Just as young children might easily lose their tempers, so too do dogs. And just as strong parents can teach their kids how to behave properly in certain situations, so too can dogs learn to behave in a more socially acceptable way.

What about those dogs who exhibit aggressive behaviors more often than not? First, know that these dogs are not the norm. Honestly, if a dog seems to "see red" all the time, he shouldn't be around the general public. Dogs like this should be in a special home or facility that can handle such specific behaviors. However, it's very rare that a dog has generalized aggressive behavior. Instead, it's usually a specific context that's the trigger.

In this chapter, I'll address the most common aggressive behaviors and how to start dealing with them. However, it's important to note that I can only address such issues on a very broad level. I would never and could never offer advice that applies across the board—aggressive behavior needs to be handled on a case-by-case basis. When it comes to repetitive or very serious aggressive behaviors, you need to work with your vet and possibly a positive trainer or animal behaviorist in your area who can help your specific dog. That being said, here's an overview of aggression.

WHY DO DOGS BEHAVE AGGRESSIVELY?

Dogs behave aggressively for a variety of reasons. Here's a breakdown:

1. Aggressive behavior usually stems from a dog being afraid and/ or not receiving enough regular exercise. In the case of fear, a dog may genuinely feel threatened and act out in the interest of

self-preservation or as a way to protect something that he values. For instance, he might bite or snap to physically neutralize the perceived threat. In the case of a lack of exercise, when dogs have pent-up energy and don't have an outlet to release it, they might get frustrated and be on edge—especially those higher-energy dogs. Their energy has to go somewhere! While some dogs might display hyperactive behavior as a way of releasing this energy, others release it by having aggressive outbursts. The good news is that exercise is likely to dramatically reduce the majority of such outbursts.

2. If a dog is in pain or has a medical condition, that might cause him to lash out. For instance, if a dog's paw hurts, he might nip at anyone who tries to touch it. One study in the *Journal of Veterinary Behavior* found that unexplained aggression in dogs was due to undiagnosed medical conditions such as hip dysplasia.[3] Also, in rare instances, some dogs may have a mental condition that causes them to behave aggressively or at least in a less predictable manner.

3. Genetics also plays a role when it comes to aggression. A dog's genes may predispose him to being fearful or overprotective or more inclined to develop certain mental illnesses. For instance, a study in *Frontiers in Psychology* found that two hormones significantly affected whether or not a dog behaved aggressively.[4] Service dogs, who are bred for their calm temperament, had higher levels of oxytocin (the feel-good hormone) than the average dog. Meanwhile, dogs who showed aggressive behaviors toward other dogs had more of the hormone vasopressin.

4. A lack of socialization and previous bad experiences can lead a dog to exhibit aggressive behaviors. If a dog has been abused in the past, he might snarl or even bite humans or other animals he doesn't know and/or trust. Sadly, who can blame him for just trying to protect himself?

5. A dog might react in a certain way simply because such behavior has worked for him in the past. For instance, if a dog guards his food bowl, he's likely doing so because he values his food and growling has kept others from taking it on previous occasions. When he growls, you might be less likely to take the food away, right? Therefore, your dog may conclude that protecting the food kept it in his possession, so he might as well continue this behavior in the future. See, aggressive behavior, like all behaviors, occurs due to a combination of life experiences, genetics, and the context in which it takes place.

6. It's equally important to address what *doesn't* cause aggressive behavior: breed! I can't tell you how much this myth bothers me. So many dog breeds, such as Pit Bulls, Rottweilers, German Shepherds, Doberman Pinschers, and Akitas, have been stereotyped as aggressive, violent dogs. This myth is so pervasive that there is actually breed-specific legislation (BSL) across the world that bans or restricts certain breeds from communities. However, the Centers for Disease Control and Prevention, the Humane Society of the United States, the American Veterinary Medical Association, the American Bar Association, and countless other reputable organizations have come out against such legislation.[5] The reason? Study after study has shown that such laws have absolutely no basis in science. For instance, a study in the *Journal of the American Veterinary Medical Association* found that breed is not a factor in dog-bite–related fatalities.[6] Also, multiple studies point out that some dogs are taught to be violent.[7] However, that has nothing to do with breed. That's all about the person raising the dog. So, while genetics may have a role in the personality of *individual* dogs of any breed, there is absolutely no hard science supporting the idea that genetics associated with aggressive behavior is widespread within specific breeds.

WHAT TO DO ABOUT AGGRESSIVE BEHAVIORS

It's critical to understand that aggression is *the most serious issue* when it comes to dog behavior. Never hesitate to seek the help of a professional positive trainer or a certified veterinary behaviorist in your area.

Remember, the first step in stopping behaviors we don't like is to keep them from occurring whenever possible. Of course, this is most important when it comes to something as potentially dangerous as aggressive behaviors. The good news is that most dogs don't just start attacking another dog or person out of the blue. When they are about to bite, they'll give you some clues that's about to happen. If you ever notice your dog displaying any of these behaviors, immediately remove him from the person, animal, or situation that's making him uncomfortable.

SIGNS OF AGGRESSIVE BEHAVIOR

Below are some signs your dog might display aggressive behavior.[8] (Also, check out the common signs that a dog is fearful, which I addressed on page 125, chapter 15, since aggressive behavior is often due to the fact that a dog is afraid.)

- Becoming very still and rigid
- Low, guttural bark
- Showing teeth
- Mouthing
- Whites of eyes exposed (known as *whale eye*)
- Wrinkled muzzle
- Turning head away
- Lips pulled back

If your dog starts acting aggressively, first take him to a vet to rule out any medical issues. This is more common than you might realize and, as I mentioned earlier, is the most probable explanation if your dog's aggressive behavior suddenly appears out of nowhere. Of course, if you think your dog is fearful, see chapter 15 on handling fear as this is likely where you need to focus your training efforts. And if your dog is overly energetic, be sure to provide him with regular exercise!

Traditionally, many dog training professionals handle dogs' aggressive tendencies by being equally aggressive. They practice dominance-based training: They yell at their dogs and hit them. They put them in alpha rolls by pinning them down on their backs. They use choke chains, prong collars, and electric shock collars in an attempt to teach them right from wrong. The logic: If your dog knows he will suffer as a result of aggressive behavior, then he is less likely to behave this way. The trouble is that this isn't how it works at all. In fact, the exact opposite is true: a survey in *Applied Animal Behaviour Science* found that when people used confrontational methods to punish their dogs, the dogs exhibited even *more* aggressive behaviors.[9] As Meghan Herron, DVM, DACVB, lead author of the study and director of the Behavioral Medicine Clinic at the Ohio State University College of Veterinary Medicine, explained so eloquently, "In almost all cases, dogs are aggressive because they are afraid and feel threatened in some way. When you use confrontational methods, you are just making yourself more threatening and increasing your dog's motivation to use aggression against you. It's like fighting fire with fire."[10]

Yes, some people who use these methods might argue that their dogs *do* decrease their aggressive behaviors. So what about those cases? That goes back to the learned helplessness explained on page 30, chapter 1. "Sometimes people can scare their dogs enough that the animals achieve a state of learned helplessness—they just sit and take it," Dr. Herron said. "Some of these dogs eventually lose this inhibition, and their aggression comes back much worse than before, as though they've snapped. And for those who don't, they remain shut down and often live in a state of perpetual fear."[11]

As if that's not bad enough, addressing aggressive outbursts *after* they occur is very counterproductive. First, it indicates a breakdown in management, which is a key to reducing all aggressive behaviors (which I cover throughout this chapter). Also, it's not teaching a dog anything.

So, what does work? You've got to show your dog what to do *instead* of having an aggressive outburst. Here's a general breakdown of the four major steps:

1. *Figure out the cause.* When dealing with aggressive behaviors in general, you have to first do your best to determine what causes those actions and when. In other words, try to understand which events or triggers are likely to cause your dog to behave aggressively. For instance, if you know that your dog is prone to snap at another dog because he's guarding a bone, then you know that you have a severe resource guarder and you can address this specific issue. Or if you know that your dog is very uneasy around people who don't follow basic etiquette when engaging a dog—which is often the case with children who might quickly rush over to dogs to hug and pet them—you can center your training efforts around these situations.

2. *Manage your dog.* Once you've determined when your dog is likely to show aggressive behaviors, you *must* be responsible about the situations that you allow your dog to be in. For instance, if you suspect that your dog is likely to become aggressive in a given situation, you need to take measures to keep him away from that specific situation until further training, desensitization, and counterconditioning has occurred. In some cases, it may be best for a dog never to be in a certain situation. For instance, if a dog has a strong history of attacking small dogs (or an apparent desire to do so), then you don't want to take such a dog to an off-leash dog park. Sure, a dog may mostly or fully recover from such behavior in some instances, but when a dog has established a history of aggressive behavior, responsible management for your dog's entire life is important. Bottom line: You must control your dog and his surroundings as responsibly as you can so that fighting, biting, or snapping is not possible. For example, make sure that your dog is always on leash in public. Also, have a crate or playpen at home to keep your dog separate from other dogs or any people he might attack. Also, as I explained on page 99, chapter 9, a humane basket muzzle can offer tremendous peace of

mind. Most importantly, always remember that your dog should *never* be in a position to hurt a person or another animal.

3. *Desensitize.* After you've managed your dog's situation, you need to desensitize your dog so that things that triggered him before become more familiar and, in turn, less likely to trigger him in the future. In other words, by setting up training exercises that safely allow you to ease your dog into situations that previously caused him to behave aggressively, he is likely to become more accepting of those things.

4. *Countercondition.* Next, you need to make deliberate, prolonged efforts to change your dog's perception of those triggers by having him associate them with things he really enjoys and likes (like reinforcement training, treats, and play!). The key is to get your dog to focus on *anything* that seems to make him happy during safely controlled training exercises.

Also, overall training is *particularly* important when it comes to managing a dog who behaves aggressively. For example, you'll need to be very committed to basic training around distractions and working on general impulse control exercises (like a surprise "leave it" and a surprise "stay"). It's pretty tough to communicate with a dog that you want him to stop attacking things if you haven't spent many months teaching your dog all of the required skills combined with lots of surprise primary sessions in a variety of situations.

Also, while I'd love to say that there is a simple cure to all moderate to severe aggressive behavior, I cannot. Even if you follow the tips in this chapter perfectly, I really want to stress the importance of responsible management if you have a dog with issues related to aggression. In other words, if a dog has established a pattern or history of acting out toward people or animals, then you must always assume he is capable of doing it again.

Lastly, I totally understand the need to resolve aggressive behavior as soon as possible, but if you want long-term success, you need to be dedicated and committed. This can take time, so be patient. Throughout the rest of this chapter, I'll show you how to implement the strategies I just explained when dealing with specific aggressive behaviors.

HANDLING RESOURCE GUARDING

Many dogs growl or snap when they think another dog or a human might take something of theirs. Such a resource might be their food, toys, sleeping area, home, or even the human they live with. We don't know why some dogs are more prone to resource guarding than others. However, it's a normal dog behavior: according to the American Society for the Prevention of Cruelty to Animals, "Wild animals who successfully protect their valuable resources—such as food, mates, and living areas—are more likely to survive in the wild than those who don't."[12]

However, when domestic dogs start growling and snapping at other dogs or people who come near their prized possessions, it stands to reason that you'd want to deal with this behavior head-on. And the good news is that you can: leading behaviorists agree that this issue is very treatable, even though shelters responding to a nationwide survey sadly reported that food aggression was the main reason they wouldn't let a dog be adopted out.[13]

So how do you handle resource guarding? You can apply the steps below whether you are trying to prevent resource guarding from becoming an issue—which is ideal—or attempting to resolve resource guarding that's already been established:

1. If you have a resource guarder on your hands, be a good manager! Don't leave things lying around that your dog is likely to protect. In other words, bring the behavior to a stop if possible. So, if your dog guards his bones, then don't leave them out and easily accessible. For each instance that guarding behavior "works" for your dog, you are that much farther away from resolving the issue. Of course, there's an exception to this: I understand that guarding food is common, and you can't just take the food away since you have to feed your dog. However, in this section I'll walk you through what to do in that case.

2. Now that you've managed the situation, it's time to set up training drills to get your dog to stop resource guarding a particular item. Let's say your dog tends to become possessive when you give him a chew toy to enjoy. Rather than simply giving him the chew

toy and then addressing the issue after an unfavorable reaction occurs, hold the toy, let him sniff it, say "Leave it," and then offer a small bit of chicken or other high-value currency. Your goal is to communicate, "I like that you politely sniffed that toy for a split second and didn't become possessive." Do this a couple dozen times in a row. If he tries to grab it, you need to take even smaller steps. For example, let him sniff the toy for a fraction of a second and follow up by giving your dog an amazing currency. Your dog is likely to reason that getting a small piece of chicken after sniffing the chew toy briefly instead of grabbing it is a pretty good deal!

3. Next, allow your dog to smell or lick the toy for a bit longer, say, two to five seconds. Again, quickly reward the desired behavior, which in this case is not becoming protective of the item. Do you see what's going on here? You are creating an alternate, *desirable* association with your dog sharing the resource with you. As a dog begins to associate sharing with getting something he likes, he'll be more open to sharing. My YouTube video with Pancake the Corgi illustrates this well. It's called *How to Stop Food Aggression/Resource Guarding in Dogs Without Force.*

4. If your dog is guarding his food bowl specifically, it's best to work on this issue *after* your dog has already eaten so he's not too hungry. Let your dog smell the bowl of food very briefly or even eat a bit and then walk near him, dropping bits of chicken or other tasty meat in his vicinity. The goal here is to reverse the association your dog might have with a person coming near his food. Whereas he might normally think, "I've got to protect my food at all costs!" you're training him to think, "When that person comes near me, they drop better food near me!" This makes your dog much less defensive *and* further creates a wonderful association with you.

5. Once your dog realizes that you are not into stealing things he values, he is far more likely to become tolerant. You could now even try picking up the food bowl for a second, giving your dog a treat if he doesn't start growling, and then setting the bowl right

back down. At any point during these exercises, if your dog does indicate that he's uncomfortable or begins to behave possessively, take a break and try again later.

In the cases above, we started with counterconditioning, which means reversing the response a dog has while in possession of a resource. The way to desensitize your dog is to do these exercises very, very often. In other words, if it truly became normal for your dog to play this game of "I get the bowl, now you get the bowl, now I get the bowl . . ." and this game results in your dog getting what he wants *and* great treats, he is likely to be much more tolerant moving forward.

By thoroughly doing exercises like this, the treats become less necessary as your dog should begin to simply behave in a less protective manner. It really is a matter of your dog learning that even though you might take things away sometimes, you very often give them back and there is nothing for him to fear.

What about when your dog has already gained possession of an item and you need to get it away from him, even though he might snap if you get too close? First, understand that you have slipped up in the management department. It's not advisable to take the object away as you are likely to escalate the situation, and your dog is more likely to experience an aggressive outburst. Remember, your intention is to literally reduce the number of instances that such outbursts occur to as close to zero as possible.

So, what should you do instead? Tossing some small pieces of meat near the object is likely to break your dog's focus and motivate him to stop guarding the item in exchange for getting the treat you tossed nearby. You can then create a small trail of treats away from the object until you can safely retrieve it. For this to work with most dogs, you need to use a very high-value treat like chicken or turkey. This exercise isn't exactly intended to train your dog as much as it is aimed at keeping you safe and regaining control of your dog's environment.

If your dog tends to protect items from other dogs, then you really need to manage this situation very well. Do not leave dogs together unsupervised if one is likely to guard things. You don't want a fight on your hands! Instead, you'll need to set up training instances where you have both dogs in a down and a stay. First, with your guarding dog, verify that *you* can easily give various items to him and then take them away without the guarding behavior occurring (which I outlined above). Again, this is one-on-one, just you and the dog. Once you are confident your dog doesn't resource guard when another dog is not in the room, then perform the same exercises we went through above while in the presence of a second dog. That second dog should be in a down and a stay across the room. If your non–resource-guarding dog does not yet know a down and a stay, you may have him in a crate or behind a gate. True, that's not ideal since you want to show all of the involved dogs how to behave, but it's an effective form of management until you can teach that dog a proper down and a stay. Practice this often and for many weeks.

The reason it's so important that your dog is reliably letting you give and take the object while in the presence of your other dog is because you must be there to promptly take the object away the moment your dog indicates that he is going into protective mode. It's as though you are saying to your offending dog, "I won't let you have that toy/bone/food/bed if you begin to protect it." Of course, always use commonsense management when feeding your dogs or giving them treats. For example, you should find that feeding your dogs in separate areas makes them less likely to guard food. Same with treats!

HANDLING GROWLING

When a dog growls in a way that isn't obviously play, we often interpret this as aggressive behavior. The thing is, growling is how a dog vocalizes concern. That's right: when a dog growls in this manner, he is communicating that he is uneasy about something. While it may be tempting to discipline growling behavior, it's best to take a step back and evaluate what might be causing your dog angst. He may be concerned that you or another dog might want to take the bone he's chewing on, or maybe your dog is uncomfortable when a stranger gets closer to him.

In other words, growling is most often your dog communicating, "I'm scared, uncomfortable, or unsure." And that's a good thing! Growling can clue you in to exactly what your dog is upset about so you can focus your training around desensitizing your dog in lighter versions of these situations. For example, if your dog is likely to growl when another dog approaches, then set up exercises that center around getting your dog used to other dogs at a safe distance where your dog is not in a position to harm another dog. Also, you'll want to provide a desirable outcome to being in such a situation with unfamiliar dogs, as is covered in depth later in this chapter. This is counterconditioning! Another example: If your dog growls whenever you get close to his food bowl, then you'll want to work through the resource guarding exercises I just went over. For now, understand that a dog who growls is most likely a dog who is communicating uneasiness (again, unless it's play growling). Knowing how to react is what will help you understand and resolve the underlying anxiety.

Bottom line: Growling may be one of the most misunderstood behaviors when it comes to dogs. That's why it's so important to understand context when a dog growls. For instance, dogs can growl during vigorous play, when they feel scared, or when they are alert and hear another dog or person approaching. Learning to understand context and what your particular dog's body language means will help you better understand the likely cause of the growling.

HANDLING DOGS FIGHTING WITHIN THE SAME HOUSEHOLD

Dogs fighting with one another in the same house is one of the most common types of aggressive behavior. There's no doubt that this can be stressful to deal with. However, keeping a cool head and having a sensible management solution along with realistic expectations goes a long way when addressing this issue. Remember, when handling virtually all forms of aggressive behavior, you'll need to follow this formula: management, desensitization, and counterconditioning.

For example, maybe you've got two dogs who don't always get along. Maybe they're friendly toward each other sometimes, but one or both dogs have aggressive outbursts occasionally. The truth is that many dogs in multidog households have spats from time to time, and these exchanges—which might include mild teeth baring and subtle growling—are normal and healthy for the most part. However, when this dog-to-dog communication escalates into full-on fights or to the point where your dogs can't even be in the same room without going at it, it has gone too far. If that's the case, then here's what you can do (after you check with your vet to make sure a medical issue isn't causing the behavior in one or both of your dogs):

1. Before you can hope to gain traction here, you must first bring a stop to the behavior and make it impossible for the dogs to fight. At first, this may mean that you need to keep them in separate rooms and alternate their access to the rest of the house while you work on refining your communication with each dog individually through increased primary training lessons of all kinds. Your dogs must understand their basic and intermediate skills very well because you can't resolve fighting if you and your dogs don't have a clear history of reliable communication. For example, let's say you've noticed that your dogs are more likely to get into a fight when in tight spaces like a hallway. In that situation, it's extremely helpful for your dogs to have a rock-solid down and a stay so that you can prevent them from finding themselves in close quarters before it happens. Or if your dogs tend to fight when something startles them (like a ringing doorbell or an abrupt knock), it's critical that you've spent time training your dogs individually to look to you when they hear the doorbell or a knock at the door. In other words, it is essential that both dogs very reliably listen to you while not in the presence of one another before you begin insisting that they listen reliably while in the same room.

2. Once you're sure your dogs do listen to you reliably when apart, your next step is to get your dogs existing peacefully in the same room together. However, don't let them actually interact just yet. This may mean setting up a large crate in your living room

so that the two dogs don't have direct access to one another. The benefit to this specific way of management is that the dogs are able to see, smell, and hear one another—all of which is fantastic for the desensitization aspect of this training approach. The more dogs are familiar with one another and the more time they can peacefully coexist in the same room (even if one is in a crate), the more progress you'll make.

3. While one dog is in the crate, work on easy stuff like "sit," "down," and "look at me" with your other dog. Reward generously when he complies. Feel free to reward your crated dog for good behavior as well. By keeping training light, easy, and enjoyable, you are creating a more favorable association with the dogs being around one another. This is counterconditioning. You accomplish a few big things here. First, you're showing your dogs that you expect them to listen to you even when they are together. Second, you're showing them that there's little need for conflict as life is a lot better for them when they listen to you instead of taking matters into their own hands and behaving impulsively.

4. If you are able to have each dog go into a down and a stay reliably while in each other's presence, or tell one dog to "Get in your crate" (if they know that skill) so that you can quickly diffuse conflicts before they arise, then you are much more likely to be able to preempt any fights between the dogs. Again, this is an example of how seamless communication with you is critical to solving this issue. (If you need to teach your dog to get in his crate or bed, check out my video on YouTube entitled *Teach Your Dog to Go to Their Bed When Asked*.)

5. As your dogs become very reliable about listening to you in these training sessions, and you feel that they are focused enough on you and not focused on interacting with each other, you are ready to train your dogs while in the same room and without a barrier. However, if you feel there is even a slight chance that they could potentially fight, take precautions and be sure to have one or both dogs wear a basket muzzle. Remember, this type of muzzle is intended only as a safety net if the unexpected does happen; if a

fight or outburst is very likely, you shouldn't have them interact quite yet. The safety and well-being of all dogs involved is always most important. Only you will know when your dogs can be together with more relaxed supervision, but steady progress is how you can measure whether or not you're on the right track.

6. What about going forward? Will you always have to be hands-on when it comes to managing your dogs together? Probably, depending on how often their scuffles occur and how serious they get. But as your dogs catch on, you ought to have to intervene less often to prevent potential altercations as they gradually become adapted to peacefully coexisting.

HANDLING DOGS FIGHTING WITH UNFAMILIAR DOGS

If your dog is less than friendly with unfamiliar dogs in public, here's what you can do:

1. Once again, management is the first key. Be sure that your dog is absolutely unable to bite or attack another dog at any time: out on walks, when you take him to the vet, or anywhere in public. As I've mentioned throughout this chapter, have your dog wear a basket muzzle while working through this issue.

2. Next, it's time to do some desensitization and counterconditioning training exercises. Get your dog used to being in the proximity of other dogs at a safe, responsible distance. This might mean doing some basic training fifty yards away or more from other dogs if your pet is particularly uneasy around other dogs. For example, doing some easy training outside the perimeter of a fenced dog park is a great place to start. Your dog can still see, hear, and sense the other dogs from far away—far enough that he's not threatened, but close enough that he can learn to associate those dogs with something positive (like fun training with you along with lots of

high-currency rewards). This, in turn, can help alter your dog's perception of what it means to be around other dogs. He might go from thinking, "Being near other dogs is stressful and scary" to "I love being near other dogs because it means I get to show off my skills and get lots of treats or playtime."

3. Work up to getting closer and closer to the fence or other barrier as your dog demonstrates progress. Sometimes resolving dog-to-dog aggressive behavior is a matter of some simple training; other times, it's much more complicated. For that reason, you must proceed cautiously and methodically.

4. If you feel like your dog is doing well, you may be at the point of letting him interact with other dogs while wearing a basket muzzle. If you decide to do this, you'll need to set up very controlled situations, ideally with an experienced positive trainer there in person to help. It's best for dogs to be off leash and in a fenced, secure area during these encounters. With some dogs—especially those who weren't socialized properly as puppies—it's just a matter of learning good social skills by being around other dogs. Your dog may benefit from seeing social cues like play bows and other greeting behaviors from other dogs so he can learn how to interact more appropriately. Should your dog react unfavorably, never hesitate to take a step back in your training.

5. Some dogs come to accept other dogs. Others may still want nothing to do with other dogs for the rest of their lives, and that's totally fine. There are plenty of dogs who do not find being around other dogs enjoyable, and we should respect this about them. Don't get me wrong: it's *never* okay for your dog to pursue another dog aggressively. However, if he can remain in a rock-solid stay or down when you encounter other dogs, that's the goal here. It doesn't matter if he wants to become best friends with the other dogs. He just needs to behave appropriately when around them. Of course, for some dogs, this issue is a lot more serious—they just *don't* behave appropriately around other dogs at all. If that's the case, don't let your dog be around other dogs at all until you work

through these issues (if possible). There are some dogs who really shouldn't be around other dogs their entire lives. However, that doesn't mean they won't make great companions for you!

HANDLING BITING AND SNAPPING AT PEOPLE

Every year, more than 4.5 million people are bitten by dogs.[14] Children are the most common victims. If your dog is snapping at people or biting them, first seek the help of a positive trainer or animal behaviorist in your area. You really want to get this behavior under control as soon as possible. If you are committed to keeping your dog and other people safe, you must also manage your dog perfectly by not putting him in situations where he is likely to bite someone. That being said, here is some very general advice on what to do:

1. Take extra precautions when teaching your dog to be more accepting of people. It is your job to make sure that your dog is absolutely not in a position to bite or snap at people at all. For instance, don't bring your dog to work, a park, or a pet supply store until you've done sufficient training to be reasonably sure that he's unlikely to bite people. Also, keep your dog in a basket muzzle any time he might encounter another person.

2. Start desensitization drills with anyone your dog seems to like, since fear of new people is the most likely explanation as to why dogs bite or snap at people. In other words, most dogs are good around people they become familiar with, so begin by getting your dog to pay attention to you in the presence of other familiar people. Basic, easy training drills like "sit" and "stay" as well as fun tricks ought to keep your dog focused on you. (See chapter 3 to learn such basic skills, and check out my YouTube channel to learn how to teach dozens of awesome tricks. *7 Dog Tricks in 5 Minutes!* is a great video to start with.) Be sure you are rewarding generously! By doing this, you are emphasizing that your dog should get into the habit of focusing his attention on you when

around other people, *and* you're teaching him that good things happen when those people are in his company.

3. Once your dog seems okay around those specific people, slowly work your way to getting your dog used to being around strangers at a distance. During these drills, you'll want to continue communicating, "Pay attention to me! I'll show you what to do, and you don't need to be worried." This is done by doing easy, familiar training drills of things you've worked on extensively in the past—such as those addressed in chapter 3—in these newer, less familiar situations. By slowly easing your dog into being around strangers at a distance, you are much more likely to make progress. If you overwhelm your dog, then you very well might hit a roadblock. The desensitization aspect of your training should be working at whatever distance your dog needs to be—where he's comfortable, relaxed, and behaving acceptably. And again, if you feel there is any chance that your dog is likely to snap or bite, be sure he is wearing a basket muzzle so that you have a safety net in place.

4. As you make progress, set up tons of counterconditioning exercises around people at safe distances. Those distances will vary depending on your individual dog. You may need to start at fifty yards away and work from there. Do basic training sessions with the aim of getting your dog into the habit of paying attention to you consistently. Work up to a stranger tossing some great treats to your dog and repeat this often. There's no need for strangers to get close to your dog during this training. It's more important that your dog simply learn to associate strangers with something good. Progress can vary from a week or so to years depending on each dog. Your patience and understanding will help things go as smoothly as possible. Naturally, the spectrum on this issue is extremely broad. Some dogs should never be trusted around strangers, while others will come to accept new people in time. My best advice is to work slowly and cautiously. Don't be in a hurry here.

HANDLING AGGRESSION TOWARD OTHER ANIMALS

For some dogs, the thrill of chasing something small is so instinctive. However, you probably don't want your pet chasing and harming small animals in your neighborhood, like cats, rabbits, ducks, chipmunks, and squirrels. Luckily, you can nip this behavior in the bud. Usually, this type of aggressive behavior isn't fear-based as is often the case with the other types of aggressive behavior discussed so far. So, I'll address this issue a little differently. Here's what you can do:

1. First, manage the situation. Make sure that you have your dog on a leash or long lead in places where he may chase and bite small animals. In that way, you can eliminate these behaviors. While working through this issue, at no point should your dog be unsupervised or uncontrolled where any small animals might be present. That means that even on potty breaks in your yard, you'll need to be with your dog and keep him on a leash.

2. How do you desensitize your dog to small animals? Practice primary training often, especially "come" and "stay" (see pages 50 and 51, chapter 3), in environments where small animals are present. If you spend a lot of time working with your dog on training in locations where animals typically pop up, and you consistently call him off those distractions, he'll come to learn that chasing things without permission is against the rules. In other words, if you prevent your dog from chasing these animals and teach him to pay attention to you instead, then you're well on your way to breaking this habit. To teach your dog how to listen when around distractions, follow the protocols on page 174 in the next chapter. I also have tons of videos teaching this skill on my YouTube channel. One of my favorites is *How to Teach Your Dog to Stay—No Matter What!*

3. By frequently keeping training fun and enjoyable (don't forget your dog's currency!), you are conditioning your dog to learn that interacting with you and listening to you is far more fun than

chasing, say, a rabbit. In other words, he'll realize that there's no need to chase animals when you are providing a more rewarding experience. Plus, your dog is learning that when he has the impulse to chase things, he should look to you for direction instead. If your dog still seems like he'd rather chase another animal than play or get a treat, then additional impulse control training is needed as well as more exposure to enticing distractions (like rabbits!) at great enough distances that you *can* get your dog's attention. Always be prepared to take a step (or more) back when your efforts don't seem to be working.

4. If your dog loves to chase small animals, I have really good news: dogs who engage in this behavior can actually make the best fetch dogs in the world. That's because fetch provides an outlet that closely mimics the thrill of the chase and the reward of catching the "prey." Also, if you play fetch with your dog regularly, you'll help mitigate his desire to chase and attack small animals because you are satisfying that desire in an appropriate way. See page 149, chapter 17, for detailed instructions on how to teach fetch.

CHAPTER 19

NOT LISTENING AROUND DISTRACTIONS

Getting your dog to readily listen to you around distractions may be one of the most challenging parts of teaching dogs. It seems like it should be easy, right? After all, if your dog has clearly demonstrated that she understands "sit" and "stay" at home or other places where she spends a lot of time, why wouldn't she just honor your requests while in the presence of human company or other dogs, on a walk, or at the park or pet supply store?

The truth is, teaching dogs to listen around distractions isn't easy at all. It requires significant work and time—probably a lot more than you might realize. There are no shortcuts. Instead, the key is practice, practice, and more practice. In this chapter, I'll explain just what to do.

WHY DON'T DOGS LISTEN AROUND DISTRACTIONS?

Why do dogs get so distracted so easily? It's simple: dogs are super-intelligent and curious about the world. Taking an interest in something out of the ordinary is what intelligent beings do. Just as people might rush to gather around a street performer doing magic tricks, dogs find things out of the ordinary worth their attention. In other words, dogs are only doing what comes naturally to them, and it's our job to teach them how to behave otherwise.

WHAT TO DO TO MAKE SURE YOUR DOG LISTENS AROUND DISTRACTIONS

While teaching your dog to listen around distractions does take a lot of time and effort, the good news is that it's pretty straightforward. Here's what you can do:

1. First, make sure you can "pause" your dog reliably! What does that mean? Just do a basic "leave it/look at me" and a "stay," which I teach on pages 49 and 51 in chapter 3. These skills are really the foundation of most types of distraction training. "Leave it" is something you use to stop your dog from investigating something or picking it up, while "stay" means keep all four paws right where they are. It's critical that you always remember to include "look at me" when you ask your dog to "leave it." Without having your dog's attention on you, it's pretty challenging to direct her and show her what you'd prefer instead. You want to ingrain in your dog's mind that she needs to look at you when she is distracted so that you can guide her to the next steps depending on the nature of the distraction. For example, if you drop a bottle of prescription pills on the floor, you'll want your dog to leave them alone as well as to look to you so that you can then tell her to stay while you pick the pills up. Or, in the case of encountering a stray, off-leash dog

in the distance, you'll want your dog's attention on you so that you can walk in another direction smoothly and concisely without your dog lunging and barking and causing a scene. So, when your dog is distracted, first "pause" her so that you can plan your next course of action.

2. Before you can reasonably expect total focus in various distracting circumstances, you must get as creative as you can on distraction training inside your house or in other very familiar environments. Virtually all introductory training lessons must be practiced, refined, and perfected in such easy places first (though we'll discuss getting your dog's focus in new environments in the next chapter).

3. As I cover on YouTube regularly, the very first distraction-focused training lesson I teach is training your dog to leave a really good treat alone. This is why I love using real meat as the distraction because it's significant enough to be *very* tempting to a dog. If your dog can leave a piece of meat alone when you ask, then she's more likely to listen to you when there are more significant distractions such as cats, squirrels, or other dogs. See page 47, chapter 3, for additional detailed instructions on this particular drill.

4. After you've achieved a reliable beginner "leave it/look at me" and "stay," your focus needs to shift to gradually making the primary lessons more challenging. For example, once your dog has mastered leaving a piece of meat alone, put an entire plate of food or your dog's favorite toy on your coffee table and practice "leave it/look at me" and "stay." Graduate to being able to place the plate or the toy on the floor (this is tougher because your dog has even easier access to the temptation) and so on. Move the plate or toy slowly back and forth while insisting that your dog leave it alone. Things that move are generally more enticing to dogs, so this is particularly challenging. With the toy, you could even squeak it a little at first and then eventually louder and more frequently.

5. Do these primary lessons several times a day at first until you are confident you can calmly say, "Leave it! Look at me!" and set a plate of food on the floor or throw an exciting toy in front of your dog while asking for a "stay," and have her comply. In other words, you want your dog experiencing the desire to pursue something and *choosing* to leave it alone, stay, and pay attention to you instead. After you've burned this concept into your dog's mind over the course of a few weeks or even months, you're ready to graduate to those surprise primary lessons.

6. As we've covered throughout this book, surprise lessons are a super-important part of preparing a dog to listen around distractions. You must extensively practice getting your dog to "leave it/look at me" and to "stay" while in a surprised state of mind. Think about it: it's one thing to have success while giving your dog ample notice and repeated opportunities to succeed while you are right there, slowly and clearly establishing that a lesson is under way. But surprise primary lessons are where your dog is given little notice. They're like pop quizzes. Since your dog is surprised, these lessons are harder for her, so be extra-generous with your rewards. Also, get creative! For example, use everyday household objects: toss a throw pillow or towel near your dog and ask for a "stay" and a "look at me." Do a surprise knock on a table or, when asking your dog to "stay," jump up and down, and act silly. You want to teach your dog to stay no matter what is going on around her. Don't wait for organic distractions to occur before you train; instead, create believable, sudden distractions. Start off easy and gradually increase the level of distractions. No matter what, make sure your dog's focus remains on you.

7. If at any point your dog becomes way too distracted, immediately take a step back and make things easier. Say your dog gets very distracted every time you turn on the blender. That would be your cue to practice a surprise stay while you hit the blend button for a split second. Reward her for even the tiniest stay. Work up to five seconds, ten seconds, and longer. Surprise training lessons are what prime your dog to have a strong foundation to draw on when

encountering distractions in real life. So, go to great lengths to do surprise "leave it" and "stay" drills often.

8. So how do you transition from surprise lessons with purposefully set-up distractions to real life? This can be a little clunky as you won't always know when a distraction is going to emerge, so prepare yourself for that. I know it's difficult to imitate major distractions like an exuberantly barking dog who suddenly appears from behind a fence. However, if your dog is very used to being surprised by you in set-up training sessions, you'll find it easier to get her attention when she's presented with these authentic, real-world distractions. Yes, it's true that you may need to encounter many organic surprises in real life before your dog starts getting used to such common things and truly generalizes listening to you in the face of all distractions in all contexts. Again, only time and practice will get you there. But you're committed! That's why you're reading this book!

9. I know I sound like a broken record, but this point is the most critical of all: teaching your dog to listen to you around distractions takes *a lot* of practice. So keep trying to distract your dog as much as possible at home. And, as I discuss in depth in the next chapter, get out there! Go to pet supply stores and practice by the perimeter of a local dog park where you can easily manipulate the distance between your dog and other dogs. When it becomes commonplace for your dog to be around distractions, those things won't be as distracting anymore.

CHAPTER 20

NOT LISTENING IN NEW ENVIRONMENTS

Teaching your dog to listen to you in new environments is one of those things that may catch you off guard. Like distraction training, training in new places is a lot more difficult than you might think as dogs do not generalize well from new environment to new environment. When you change a variable, you need to take a few steps back in your training. In this case, that variable is the environment itself. So, if your dog acts crazy every time you go somewhere new in public—or seems to forget everything you've taught him and worked on at home—you're not alone! Lots of dogs are like this.

The only way to truly prepare a dog to listen in lots of places is to spend plenty of time in different places. Of course, this takes a lot of time and effort. As soon as you can take your dog in public—which for puppies is after your vet gives permission and for older dogs is usually right away—commit to taking him to lots of places *often,* on leash. If your dog is extra-hyper in new places and can't seem to focus, make sure you exercise him before you leave the house.

Always keep in mind that if you find your dog isn't listening to you in new places, it's because he simply hasn't been adequately prepared yet. It's not that your dog has forgotten how to listen to you; it's that he is too overwhelmed by his surroundings to focus on doing what you are asking.

This is normal, and you'll get past it by following the advice in this chapter. There is a lot to see, hear, smell, and experience from your dog's point of view, and it's your responsibility to show him the world and teach him that he still needs to listen to you no matter where he is!

WHY DON'T DOGS LISTEN IN NEW ENVIRONMENTS?

Dogs really experience the world so differently than we do. Their olfactory system is far more sophisticated than ours. They can hear amazingly well, too. In other words, you are competing with distractions you don't even realize are there! Imagine stepping from your front door into a festive carnival. Just like that, you are inundated with so many stimulating sights, smells, and sounds. Now, imagine being, say, four years old and trying to focus on reciting your ABC's upon entering such an environment. You'd likely be more into everything going on around you than you would be on mundane things like basic preschool stuff, right? It's the same way for dogs.

WHAT TO DO TO MAKE SURE YOUR DOG LISTENS IN NEW ENVIRONMENTS

It takes time to desensitize a dog to exciting environments (which may be all environments for some dogs!). The only way to truly satisfy a dog's curiosity is to let him explore these places as often as you can early in your training. Even if your dog is older and has never benefited from training like this, it's not too late! Now is the time to teach your dog about all the different types of places, like parks, stores, sidewalks, cars, friends' and relatives' houses, and so on. Here's how:

1. Budget at least two days a week where you go to one or more of these places for two to three hours at a time. So often when we are taking our dogs somewhere, it's somewhere that they haven't heavily explored before and we might be in a hurry, as in the case of getting pet food from the store or taking a walk down a different street than usual. Instead, you need to factor in time for serious, dedicated training. Whenever your dog lacks lots of time in a new place, he needs significant time to take it in and check it out.

2. Your dog is most likely *not* going to listen to you in new places as well as he does at home. It's as though training in new places lags a few weeks behind your at-home training. This is perfectly normal and expected. However, once you've given your dog ample opportunities to explore these places, you should find that he chills out a little. While he still may be interested in the new environment, after a few hours, he will probably be much more likely to adapt and perhaps even take some direction from you like "sit" or "stay." This is *exactly* what you've been waiting for! Your dog is finally receptive, albeit not as reliable as at home. But now that your dog has adapted and has demonstrated a willingness to listen to you, you need to work on going over the basics and other things that you've taught him. Whereas before, your goal was to let your dog take in the environment, now you're getting him to pay less attention to the environment and more attention to you.

3. When you train in new places, make sure that you bring high-value currencies for the first several months of training. You are competing with so many distractions in new environments that having something amazing with you (such as chicken or a favorite toy that your dog *loves*) is critical. Once your dog sits for the first time in a new place, reward enthusiastically, as though he just sat for the first time in his life. While "sit" might not be breaking new ground, sitting while in a new place is a new behavior, and that warrants optimal reinforcement! The more enjoyable the outcome to a given behavior, the more likely your dog is to repeat it in the future.

4. In short, your goal is to make various environments so familiar that your dog actually begins to pay attention to you at those places as he does at home. If your dog is extremely unresponsive in the places where you want him to listen, then up to a year of steady exposure and gradual training is probably necessary. On the other hand, some dogs catch on a lot faster. There are no quick fixes to this, but through lots of practice, you can do it!

I want to share a personal story that really conveys exactly how to teach a dog to listen to you in a new environment. When I first got my dog, Venus, I made a commitment to train her to be a competition Frisbee dog and planned to participate in an annual, high-profile Frisbee dog competition in Atlanta's Piedmont Park. For those of you not familiar with competition Frisbee dogs, it's about a lot more than teaching a dog to chase and catch a Frisbee. In the challenging freestyle portion, dogs are taught to do stunning vaults off of their handler's body and backflips. They'll catch several Frisbees in rapid succession and even catch two separate Frisbees in a single throw. (As far as I know, Venus is the only dog to have caught three separate Frisbees in a single throw as of the writing of this book.) What I love about it is that you can be as creative as you'd like with your routine.

In terms of audience size, this particular competition is one of the most attended Frisbee dog competitions around. As teams compete throughout the day, there are thousands of people gathered around the competition field at any given moment. Talk about distractions!

Since I was planning to do my first freestyle routine with Venus at this competition, I made it a point to practice with her in super-busy areas with lots of pedestrians. Most of these practices were at fields near my house—we'd get out there bright and early about four days a week. However, at least once a week, I'd make the twenty-minute drive down to Piedmont Park to practice on the *exact* patch of grass where the competition would be held several months later. If the weather was nice, you could count on tons of people being at Piedmont Park all weekend long. The way I saw it, the competition was in our hometown and I was going to get every advantage I could by setting up conditions that mirrored those of the competition day as closely as possible.

Along with the location, I also tried to prepare Venus by proactively replicating other competition conditions as best as I could. I went as far as bringing a portable CD player playing the music that we'd perform to. Of course, there would still be even more distractions at the competition, like a much bigger audience, louder music, other dogs, and lots of smells. So, I couldn't do everything.

But I *could* focus on creating distractions and training her to always look to me no matter what caught her attention. For instance, she had a weakness for soccer balls, so if people were kicking a ball back and forth, I knew she might bolt. And she did so twice on those first two visits. In the following weeks, I'd bring my own soccer ball and have Venus on a long lead so that I could practice getting her attention off the soccer ball and back on our routine. I'd do a Frisbee sequence and kick a ball unexpectedly, asking her for a "stay" and a "look at me" while going on with the routine. If I could call Venus off of a soccer ball, then I could get her to focus under just about any other condition. Since I had already built solid communication with her, it was a pretty easy task to get her to stop getting distracted by the ball. She quickly learned that she still had to pay attention to me.

Over the next several months, we became staples at Piedmont Park every weekend. It was great! Then, in spring 2004, we entered our first Frisbee freestyle competition. I was terrified, but I trusted that we did everything we could to prepare. The music started, our routine was under way, and the rumble of those first "oohs" and "ahhs" as I warmed Venus up with figure eights between my legs was something that wasn't there before in practice! I was highly aware that thousands of people were watching us. Talk about nerve-racking! The first throw was a twenty-yard throw. Venus didn't miss a beat. She caught it, and I'll never forget how proud I was of her at that moment. With each catch, the crowd cheered. We ended our routine with a "back stall." That's where you hunch over, making your back horizontal with the ground, and your dog jumps up and balances on your back. Venus sat up into the best "sit pretty." The crowd erupted louder for her than any other dog of the day and gave us a standing ovation. They loved it! And so did the judges, as we took first place in the competition. Some might call it beginner's luck, and they might be right—but I think preparation had a lot to do with it, too!

As fun as it is to relive this story, I detail it here only to underscore how important it is to give your dog the opportunity to succeed in training. While you may not be so interested in competing with your dog in such activities, the same concepts I addressed with Venus apply when you want to take your dog to new environments. You must still work with him and prepare him so that he knows exactly what to do.

CHAPTER 21

NOT LISTENING OFF LEASH

Sure, it would be great to have your dog listen to you perfectly whether or not she's on leash. However, people are generally *way* too quick to give their dog such privileges. I see this most with new dogs, especially puppies. Puppies, by nature, tend to stay near people off leash. We are, after all, a great resource for food, play, and attention. It also seems as though puppies haven't yet realized that there is so much of the world to explore, so they stay close. And what do their people then often assume? "Wow, looks like my dog is good off leash, and I don't have to have her on one anymore!" I promise you, that's not the case. Regardless of age, most dogs need to be on leash for a long time, if not indefinitely, unless you properly train them to be off leash.

If your dog is getting away or bolting out the front door and you are looking for an answer as to how to get her back, you must take a massive step backward on your training and tightly control the environment. The leash is the most valuable tool to help you do just that. There are absolutely no excuses when it comes to keeping your dog safe, so make sure your dog is *never* in a position to get away from you and put herself in a potentially dangerous situation. And until your dog is reliable on leash, she has no business being off leash, unless in a perfectly safe environment such as your house or fenced-in yard. However, you can get your dog to listen to you off leash. In this chapter, I explain how.

WHY DON'T DOGS LISTEN WHILE OFF LEASH?

Most dogs are free spirits and live in the moment. If they see something interesting or exciting, they'll often investigate those things without regard to what you want. They don't understand that a car can hit them if they run toward another dog across the street, nor do they contemplate that they could get lost if they focus on a scent trail taking them halfway across town. Off-leash training takes months and months, and, again, you shouldn't even place an emphasis on it until your dog listens to you *very* reliably while on leash. For instance, if your dog won't easily sit or stay in any particular environment, you're not yet ready to begin off-leash training in that environment.

WHAT TO DO TO MAKE SURE YOUR DOG LISTENS WHILE OFF LEASH

A huge part of phasing in off-leash training is having *perfect* control of the environment, which is why I recommend getting a twenty-foot lead leash. The lead allows you to simulate off-leash conditions because you're able to interact with your dog at a greater distance. It also eliminates risk—think of it as a safety net in the event your dog does not listen to you. Here's what you can do:

1. Do tons of training in lots of different places while your dog is on the longer lead. Practice all of the skills you've taught at home in these places. Have your dog sit, stay, and lie down (see chapter 3 for a refresher on basic skills), and maybe do a trick or two if your dog knows any.

2. Place a strong emphasis on distance training. For example, ask your dog to sit and stay from one foot away, then five feet away, and then up to twenty feet over the course of a few weeks. Go gradually and only increase difficulty with distance training as your dog becomes very reliable.

3. Now it's time to add distractions. Since you're adding a new variable—the distractions—start close to your dog (later you'll gradually increase the distance). Get super-creative with the distractions you implement in your training now. Be sure to bring along your dog's absolute favorite things to use as distractions. For example, if your dog loves a squeaky toy, make it a goal to teach her to stay while you heavily animate and squeak the toy. Work up to throwing the toy as your dog demonstrates she can hold a stay. Reward with the same toy, a different toy, or treats, accordingly. By the way, if you're wondering about using the favorite toy as a distraction *and* a reward, it's fine. The bottom line is that your dog can play with the toy when you give permission, but she must leave it alone when you ask.

4. If you've got it in you, jump up and down and wave your arms while squeaking the toy and vocalizing in a high-pitched voice! Yes, onlookers will think you're insane, but that just goes with the territory. The point I'm making is that you need to use your imagination and do your absolute best to simulate highly enticing distractions so that when your dog is presented with something she views as exciting in the real world, she'll have the training to know what to do: listen to you. This is the time to go for it and give your dog everything you've got. If your dog "fails" two times in a row and goes for the distractions, you're not there yet, so go slower and practice more.

5. Make these training exercises more challenging by focusing on gradually increasing your training bubble. No next step should be difficult for your dog. You are working toward being able to throw all kinds of distractions at your dog while farther away from her. Yes, you are now combining the distance training with the distraction training. The reason we're focusing so heavily

on extending the distance is because it's a higher level of communication. If your dog listens to you at twenty feet away—and when distracted—then she's on her way to listening when you're playing fetch at the park off leash and something unexpected happens (like she sees a rabbit in the distance!).

6. Assuming the above training is going well, set up some surprise primary sessions. See if you can get friends or kids at the park to run around in front of your dog a few feet away while you ask your dog to stay. Even have them toss treats near your dog. At the same time, practice "leave it" and "look at me." By having real strangers do things that are highly distracting in practice, you are truly preparing your dog. The fact is that your set-up training drills should be *more* distracting than anything you are likely to encounter in real life. See, in these set-up moments, your attention is on your dog in a way that's hard to duplicate if you wait for both you and your dog to be surprised. Your results will only be as good as the training, so be thorough over a course of many months on this type of advanced training and prioritize being more and more unpredictable as your dog improves.

7. One of the toughest parts of off-leash training is finding truly new, unfamiliar places to rehearse in. Once your dog is doing really well at your regular training spots, your challenge will be to seek out fenced-in areas that your dog is unfamiliar with, like ball fields first thing in the morning on a weekday (you'll be less likely to encounter other events going on during these times). Still, keep your dog on a lead as you must be able to prevent relapses. Ideally, your dog shouldn't realize the area is completely fenced as she likely won't if you don't frequent the location. Now you have a double-controlled environment, the leash and the fence, so you'll have more flexibility to practice more lifelike training drills like "come" from farther distances or "stay" while you stand twenty feet away and launch a Frisbee, for example. This is how you test your off-leash training.

8. During these specific types of training sessions, your dog must be held to the standard of listening unwaveringly. Once your dog is consistently listening to you at significant distances of ten feet or more, you can drop the leash and practice as normal. If your dog does have a relapse, it's far easier to catch her when she has a twenty-foot lead attached to her. When you are able to flawlessly communicate with your dog while the leash is attached, but without your having to hold it, you are then ready to take the lead off. But remember, you still have the added protection of a fenced area. Be careful here though. Avoid making the assumption that, since your dog is doing well with the long lead dangling from her collar harness, she'll now listen when you detach it. It doesn't work that way. Dogs are smart and they *will* notice the difference. In other words, your dog is likely to notice she's no longer attached to the leash. For this reason, start from the beginning when entering this new off-leash phase of training. Work on basic training while your dog is off leash *at close range*. Next, start with smaller distractions only and work up to greater distractions over the next several sessions. If at any point your dog becomes less cooperative, that's your cue to put that long lead right back on. You'll also need to be more thorough with your training and try again once your dog has advanced. However, if you've gotten to this point in your training, you are most likely going to succeed, so stay the course!

9. I cannot stress this next point enough: this type of training should be done for months and tested over and over again before you try to take your dog's leash off in a real-life situation. You'll want to know that your dog listens while off leash (but in a variety of fenced, secure environments) in the morning, afternoon, and evening; after eating breakfast; on days when she's feeling extra-energetic; and on days when she's less enthusiastic about training. All moods, all conditions, all of the time. You want to be as certain as possible that your dog isn't going to run away when you, say, take her on a hike without her leash on. It's just not worth the risk.

10. Not all dogs will excel at off-leash training, and progress might be very slow for some, especially those high-energy dogs. These dogs tend to be ultra-curious about their world, so it takes a special commitment to get them to this higher level of training. It's not for lack of intelligence, but rather due to their love of life! However, with appropriate exercise just before training sessions, they are far more likely to succeed. Also keep in mind that some dogs will never be okay off leash, and that's fine, too. Only you will know when the time is right to let your dog off leash in certain situations, if ever.

HANDLING CHASING CARS

If your dog is chasing cars, you are a long way off from off-leash training. Instead, your focus needs to be on basic training on leash in the presence of cars for an extended period of time, depending on your dog's progress. If your dog is highly reactive to cars, then begin in slow traffic areas. Focus on practicing your dog's general training routine with cars in the distance. Assuming your dog listens well here, work up to doing desensitization and counterconditioning exercises in the presence of more significant traffic. As cars become less enticing simply due to frequent exposure, and as you reinforce good behavior with rewards when your dog does react well, you'll be closer to getting your dog to listen to you reliably. Don't rush this process. And remember, of course, that dogs should never really have access to moving cars no matter how well they're trained. For more on this, see my video *Train Your Dog to Stop Chasing and Lunging at Cars: Where to Start*.

HANDLING RUNNING AWAY

A lot of dogs like to bolt out the front door whenever you open it. This is a scary, dangerous habit—one you've got to nip in the bud right away. Dogs quickly learn that the moment your hand goes toward the doorknob they are about to gain access to the outdoors. For some dogs, you might notice that even grabbing your keys tips them off that the door is about to open. I have great videos on YouTube that walk you through getting your dog to stay when you open a door leading to the outside, such as *How to Stop Your Dog from Running Out of the Front Door! Stay While Distracted*. Graci the Portuguese Water Dog was my guest in that video—she had lots of energy and the most inviting personality. Her training session and results were very typical of what most people can expect in just one or two lessons. I also have some basic advice on how to handle this:

1. First, be sure that your "stay" training is very solid during your primary training and surprise primary training sessions. See page 51, chapter 3, for a refresher on teaching this skill.

2. Next, practice "stay" at various doors leading to the outdoors, but keep your dog on leash and take special care to keep her from running out of the door. Remember, start very, very small. Tap the doorknob with your finger for a second and reward if your dog stays. If not, take a step back and practice basic "stay" training under conditions that are easier for your dog (such as nowhere near the front door). Repeat this exercise five or six times.

3. If all goes well, ask for a sit or a down and a stay, and grasp the doorknob for a second or two. Don't turn it yet. Acknowledge your dog's successful stay and reward accordingly.

4. Next, wiggle the doorknob briefly while encouraging a "stay" and reward. Work up to cracking the door open a centimeter and for a brief moment. Close the door. Then work up to being able to keep the door open for just a couple of seconds. Close the door and reward your dog for learning this life-saving skill.

5. Once your dog holds a thirty-second stay with the door open (and on leash), phase in the distraction training outlined in chapter 19. Start small and work up to more challenging sessions. The major variable change here is that the door is open. Whenever changing a variable (such as adding an open door to the mix), keep everything else as easy as you can for your dog at first and prioritize reinforcing the behavior you are there to teach. In this case, that's staying at the door. Gradually, make these training drills more elaborate. For instance, throw distractions outside while you ask for a "stay." Use a combination of food, toys, and other temptations to "proof" your training. If your dog holds a "stay" when you throw her favorite toy or bits of chicken out the front door, she's more likely to stay when the door is open in real life and there aren't major distractions.

Needless to say, it's extremely important that you control the environment flawlessly here. You are not guaranteed that your dog will be safe or that you will get her back if you let down your guard and she runs out the front door. In short, make sure that your dog does not *ever* have the opportunity to slip out of the door. This skill is so important that I recommend you do these training exercises extremely often over two months or more. If you make this a priority to teach, your dog will have this concept down pat quickly.

CHAPTER 22

NOT LISTENING
WITHOUT TREATS

A logical question a lot of people ask me is, "Do I always have to use treats and other rewards?" As you know by now, teaching a dog how to behave in a variety of different situations and places is a fairly in-depth process. So, while you may not have to reward liberally forever, you do need to use rewards longer than you might think. Remember that every time you change a variable on a dog (for example, the environment), this is very likely to make the training exercise more difficult since the conditions surrounding the training experience have changed. Rewards are what help you efficiently communicate with your pet in all sorts of places and situations.

To be extra-clear, let's just recap this point: don't assume that just because your dog picks up on something like "leave it" in a single training session or two that that means he knows how to leave things alone in all other situations. Real dog training requires contextual training in specific conditions, both set up and organic, over a *significant amount of time*— certainly throughout the first year of training, regardless of your dog's age, and longer if you continue to teach him newer, more advanced concepts.

Yes, it's necessary to dole out lots of praise, rewards, and fun around the most basic proper behaviors for a while. However, as your dog matures and learns, you don't have to emphasize rewards for basic things as those behaviors become second nature.

Think about coaching an experienced thirteen-year-old baseball player versus a seven-year-old beginner player. For the veteran player, you would have higher expectations and not focus on praising every little success during easier aspects of the game. For instance, if the seven-year-old fields an easy grounder, you'd probably cheer and shout and say something like, "Great job!" If the older child made the same play, you might not even cheer at all since such plays are commonplace and even expected at that point. That's what it's like teaching dogs!

In this chapter, I'll go over some key things you need to know about how often to reward your dog at first during primary training sessions and how to gradually get your dog to listen to you reliably even when not being rewarded.

WHY DON'T DOGS LISTEN WITHOUT TREATS AND OTHER REWARDS?

You can't expect a dog who receives a treat every single time you ask for a particular behavior to continue that behavior when you suddenly stop giving rewards cold turkey. I'm not saying you'll have to use rewards forever, but you've got to wean your dog off of them gradually. This is the concept behind intermittent reinforcement, which I'll cover later in this chapter. However, before I get to that, it's critical to understand the importance of finding the right *rate of reinforcement* during each training session. Doing that, in turn, helps you determine exactly when you need to use rewards and when you can get by without them.

THE IMPORTANCE OF THE RATE OF REINFORCEMENT

The rate at which you reward your dog is a super-important variable during any given training session. When it comes to the *rate of reinforcement*, I'm talking about how rapidly you reward a dog for a certain behavior within an individual training lesson. Let's say you are teaching your dog to stay while you walk away from him. At first, you'll need to back away just a foot or two, and then rush back and reward your dog. But that doesn't mean that the training session is over. You now want to seal this behavior in and heavily reinforce it while your dog is paying attention. In other words, repeat this several times in a row in fast succession—maybe five repetitions in twenty seconds. You are literally trying to get in as many reps as possible, so there should be some hustle to your method just after you begin to achieve initial progress on something new. These rapid-fire rewards in fast succession might look like over-rewarding to the novice. However, there is a method behind this madness, and that is a very conscious, deliberate effort to imprint desired behavior in your dog. (That's why I recommend using very tiny, high-quality treats like real meat!) This liberal rewarding style is particularly valuable when introducing new concepts or for when you need to take a step back and repair a once reliable behavior. It's also critical anytime you change a variable in your training, like asking your dog to stay at a park he's never been to before.

As your dog's behaviors such as "sit," "stay," and proper leash walking become habits, slow the rate of reinforcement down a bit. For example, you might find yourself only rewarding twice on a one-hour walk with your dog in the later stages of your leash walking training, whereas at first you may be rewarding every few seconds. Understanding the cadence and rhythm of rewarding your dog is something that comes with time, but remember that the newer or more difficult something is, the faster your rate of reinforcement should be. The more reliable the behavior becomes, the slower your rate of reinforcement.

Be flexible when it comes to determining the rate during an individual training session. Sometimes your dog may be frustrated, and you need to make things more enjoyable. In such a case, up your rate of reinforcement. Other times you may have incredible momentum on something and you suspect you can get by with a slower rate of rewarding. That's fine, too! It's important that you carefully reconsider the speed at which you reward during every lesson. You'll see lots of examples of this in my videos on YouTube.

WHAT TO DO WHEN YOUR DOG DOESN'T LISTEN WITHOUT TREATS OR OTHER REWARDS

So when can you wean off treats and other rewards? That's where intermittent reinforcement comes into play! Here's the concept:

1. When first teaching something new or changing up a training condition, reward your dog almost 100 percent of the time he's successful. However, as your dog starts to get the hang of things, lower your rewards to 70 percent; then during another training session, drop it down to 40 percent. Then, maybe up your rewards to 50 percent. Doing so will likely make behaviors *more* reliable moving forward—in fact, the science behind intermittent reinforcement is strong.[1] It's this same type of learning that makes things like gambling and video games so addictive—you only succeed *sometimes* and that, in turn, makes you *more* likely to continue to participate and become even more determined. When teaching your dog, the goal is to keep things just interesting enough to keep him really engaged. The less able your dog is to decipher a pattern in when you reward and the more uncertain he is as to whether or not he will receive a reward, the more likely he is to do what you are asking.

2. While your dog is new to learning how to behave in the world, it's so important to go out of your way to provide great outcomes to desired behaviors and to do so very often. It's a little difficult to say exactly when you don't need to reward as it is such a subtle, gradual process. However, as your dog starts doing his basics more and more reliably, then you are on track to begin phasing out rewards in day-to-day training.

3. Should you ever get rid of treats altogether? Well, that kind of depends on the behavior. In my experience, I don't see that it's necessary to reward on basic behaviors forever, unless you want to do so. If you've done a good job of rewarding for the first year of training, then these basic behaviors should be pretty reliable. In the case of my dogs, I still frequently reward them for tricks and more advanced behaviors. My advice is to experiment using

varying rates of reinforcement and intermittent rewarding according to your dog's success with a particular skill and adjust these factors based on your dog's progress over time. In the way that parents still reinforce their love and pride for their grown children by giving them presents on their birthdays, picking up the check at a restaurant, and praising their new job promotion, so too is it a good idea to give your dog extra rewards for consistent good behavior periodically and well into adulthood. I suspect, though, that most of you are very likely to do this without my advice. Dogs are so authentic and genuine that it's hard not to let them know how much we appreciate them throughout their lives.

CONCLUSION

You probably bought this book because you wanted greater insight into how to better understand your dog and to learn how to teach her right from wrong. Your dog might have a particular issue like barking, play biting, or chewing that you want to stop immediately. Or maybe your dog has started showing aggressive behaviors, and you want to nip them in the bud before they escalate any further. The good news is that the very fact that you read this book shows that you care—and having that loving relationship with your dog is the critical foundation that will help you work through any issue.

I hope that through this book, I've managed to help you keep your expectations in line with reality. Remember, just as with humans, no dog is perfect. Sure, dogs are super-intelligent and very capable of extraordinary things, but they're not robots. I've known some pretty incredible dogs in my life, but every single one of them had little quirks. My first dog, Venus, is a great example of this—she was brilliant and phenomenal in so many ways. However, she was also always scared of thunderstorms and never very social with other dogs or people. And that was perfectly fine. In fact, if you ask me, I think dogs' imperfections are what make them so lovable and charming. Sure they're goofy and overly enthusiastic at times, and they can certainly be a little sneaky, too. That's what makes them so irresistible!

Also, I hope you've learned that you need to train your dog as *you* want her to behave. You may find that there are certain behaviors that don't bother you so much, like digging or jumping on you when you come home. Ultimately, you are the one who needs to decide what you are okay with. If you don't mind your dog jumping on the furniture, that's fine! If digging in the backyard doesn't bother you, that's fine, too! There are no rules other than the ones you want your dog to learn to follow (and those protecting the safety of your dog and other animals and people, of course!).

Keep in mind that some issues take longer to address than others, and some dogs learn faster than others. But after balancing all of these factors, remember that nobody knows your dog like you do and nobody is better equipped to teach her than you! As you work through your dog's behavioral issues together, pick your battles as you would with a child and prioritize the training that you think is most important at that time. Trying to take on too much too quickly only leads to frustration between you and your dog, so stretch out that training time accordingly and always enjoy it. Remember that any progress is fantastic!

My first three dogs—Venus, Supernova, and Alpha Centauri—have sadly passed on, but I can now reflect on their lives and all of the training I did with them over the years. What I've come to realize is that while it may have felt at times that I was doing all the teaching, the biggest lessons were actually the ones that *I* learned from my dogs. I admire their genuine, lifelong innocence. I'm amazed at how they never dwelled on mistakes and envious of how they really seemed to live their lives to the fullest. Even simple pleasures like chewing a bone or playing a game of fetch or chase appeared to bring them *so* much happiness.

However, it was their ability to love unconditionally that gets me the most. Dogs never hesitate to show you just how much they care about you. They're always loyal. So, regardless of how hyper, loud, or annoying your dog might be from time to time, I'm sure you'll agree that the trade-off is so worth it as there's nothing quite like being the recipient of a dog's affection, friendship, and love. Dogs make our lives richer. We are better because of them.

The Dog Training Revolution has grown beyond belief in recent years. Because of people like you, the movement has unstoppable momentum. I want to express my personal gratitude to you for committing to teach your dog thoughtfully and compassionately and for taking the time to achieve a richer, fuller relationship with her. I hope this book helps you to continue doing just that.

ENDNOTES

INTRODUCTION

1. J. Y. Kwan and M. J. Bain, "Owner Attachment and Problem Behaviors Related to Relinquishment and Training Techniques of Dogs," *Journal of Applied Animal Welfare Science* 16, no. 2 (2013): 168–183. www.ncbi.nlm.nih.gov/pubmed/23544756.

2. "Shelter Intake and Surrender," American Society for the Prevention of Cruelty to Animals, accessed December 1, 2017. www.aspca .org/animal-homelessness/shelter-intake-and-surrender.

3. M. Savage, " 'Cruel' Electric Shock Pet Training Collars to Be Banned in England," *Guardian,* March 10, 2018. www.theguardian .com/world/2018/mar/11/animal-cruel-electric-shock-pet-training-collar-ban-england; "Electric Shock Collars," Kennel Club, accessed December 5, 2017. www.thekennelclub.org.uk/our-resources/ kennel-club-campaigns/electric-shock-collars.

4. M. E. Herron et al., "Survey of the Use and Outcome of Confrontational and Nonconfrontational Training Methods in Client-Owned Dogs Showing Undesired Behaviors," *Applied Animal Behaviour Science* 117, no. 1–2 (2009): 47–54. http: //binalunzer.com/Links_ files/aversive-stimulation.pdf; "Dominance and Dog Training," Association of Professional Dog Trainers, accessed December 15, 2017. apdt.com/resource-center/dominance-and-dog-training; "Position Statement: The Use of Punishment for Behavior Modification in Animals," American Veterinary Society of Animal Behavior, accessed December 15, 2017. avsab.org/wp-content/ uploads/2018/03/Punishment_Position_Statement-download_- _10-6-14.pdf.

CHAPTER 1: TEN ESSENTIALS FOR A WELL-BEHAVED DOG

1. D. A. Raichlen et al., "Wired to Run: Exercise-Induced Endocanna-binoid Signaling in Humans and Cursorial Mammals with Implications for the 'Runner's High,'" *Journal of Experimental Biology* 215, no. 8 (2012): 1331–1336. jeb.biologists.org/content/215/8/1331.

2. M. Nagasawa et al., "Oxytocin-Gaze Positive Loop and the Coevolution of Human-Dog Bonds," *Science* 348, no. 6232 (2015): 333–336. science.sciencemag.org/content/348/6232/333.

3. K. Tiira and H. Lohi, "Early Life Experiences and Exercise Associate with Canine Anxieties," *PLoS ONE* 10, no. 11 (2015).

4. *Dogs: Their Secret Lives,* "Survey Results Revealed: Are Dogs Who Play, Better Behaved?" video, 2:01. www.markevans.co.uk/television/dogs-secret-lives.

5. M. E. P. Seligman and S. Maier, "Failure to Escape Traumatic Shock," *Journal of Experimental Psychology* 74, no. 1 (1967): 19.

6. J. Ciribassi. Interview by Dina Roth Port, May 8, 2018.

CHAPTER 2: WHY DOGS BEHAVE "BADLY"

1. L. Ostojić et al., "Are Owners' Reports of Their Dogs' 'Guilty Look' Influenced by the Dogs' Action and Evidence of the Misdeed?" *Behavioural Processes* 111 (2015): 97–100. www.sciencedirect.com/science/article/pii/S0376635714003210.

2. V. Ward, "A Dog's Guilty Look Is Just a Myth, Experts Claim," *The Telegraph,* August 25, 2015.

3. A. Horowitz, "Disambiguating the 'Guilty Look': Salient Prompts to a Familiar Dog Behavior," *Behavioural Processes* 81, no. 3 (2009): 447–452.

4. L. D. Mech, "Alpha Status, Dominance, and Division of Labor in Wolf Packs," *Canadian Journal of Zoology* 77 (1999): 1196–1203.

5. L. D. Mech., "Outdated Notion of the Alpha Wolf," L. David Mech website, accessed January 10, 2018. www.davemech.org/news.html.

6. F. D. McMillan, "Behavioral and Psychological Outcomes for Dogs Sold as Puppies Through Pet Stores and/or Born in Commercial Breeding Establishments: Current Knowledge and Putative

Causes," *Journal of Veterinary Behavior: Clinical Applications and Research* 19 (2017): 14–26.

7. "How Cruel Breeding Hurts Dogs," American Society for the Prevention of Cruelty to Animals, accessed January 15, 2018. www.aspca.org/barred-from-love/puppy-mills-101/how-cruel-breeding-hurts-dogs.

8. I. Zapata et al., "Genetic Mapping of Canine Fear and Aggression," *BMC Genomics* 17, no. 1 (2016).

9. K. L. Overall. Interview by Dina Roth Port, May 29, 2018.

10. "Literature Review on the Welfare Implications of Socialization of Puppies and Kittens," American Veterinary Medical Association, 2015, accessed January 20, 2018.

11. "AVSAB Position Statement on Puppy Socialization," American Veterinary Society of Animal Behavior, 2008, accessed January 20, 2018. avsab.org/wp-content/uploads/2018/03/Puppy_Socialization_Position_Statement_Download_-_10-3-14.pdf.

CHAPTER 4: BARKING

1. G. Elert, *The Physics Factbook: Frequency Range of Dog Hearing*, accessed January 25, 2018. hypertextbook.com/facts/2003/TimCondon.shtml.

CHAPTER 6: JUMPING UP

1. "Position Statement on the Use of Dominance Theory in Behavior Modification of Animals," American Veterinary Society of Animal Behavior, 2008, accessed February 1, 2018. avsab.org/wp-content/uploads/2018/03/Dominance_Position_Statement_download-10-3-14.pdf; J. Lee-St. John, "Dog Training and the Myth of Alpha-Male Dominance," *Time*, July 30, 2010, accessed January 15, 2018. http://content.time.com/time/health/article/0,8599,2007250,00.html.

2. "How to Teach Your Dog Not to Jump," WebMD veterinary reference from ASPCA Virtual Pet Behaviorist, accessed February 5, 2018. pets.webmd.com/dogs/guide/dogs-jumping-training-tips-not-do—1.

CHAPTER 9: LEASH PULLING

1. J. Ciribassi. Interview by Dina Roth Port, May 8, 2018.

CHAPTER 12: DIGGING

1. "Dig This: How to Get Your Dog to Stop Digging," Humane Society of the United States, accessed February 25, 2018. www.humanesociety.org/animals/dogs/tips/digging.html.

2. A. Benjamin and K. Slocombe, "Who's a Good Boy?!" Dogs Prefer Naturalistic Dog-Directed Speech, *Animal Cognition* 21, no. 3: 353–364.

CHAPTER 13: EATING POOP

1. "Why Dogs Eat Poop and How to Stop It," American Kennel Club, 2015, accessed February 16, 2018. www.akc.org/expert-advice/health/common-conditions/why-dogs-eat-poop.

2. "Why Do Dogs and Puppies Eat Poop," petMD, accessed March 1, 2018. www.petmd.com/dog/puppycenter/health/evr_dg_why_do_puppies_eat_poop.

3. B. L. Hart et al., "The Paradox of Canine Conspecific Coprophagy," *Veterinary Medicine and Science* 4, no. 2 (2018): 106–114.

CHAPTER 14: HUMPING

1. "Common Dog Behavior Issues: Mounting and Masturbation," American Society for the Prevention of Cruelty to Animals, accessed February 6, 2018.

2. Ibid.

CHAPTER 15: FEARS AND PHOBIAS

1. S. Borns-Weil. Interview by Dina Roth Port, May 14, 2018.

2. G. M. Landsberg and S. Denenberg, "Behavior Problems of Dogs," *Merck Veterinary Manual*, accessed April 1, 2018. www.merckvetmanual.com/behavior/normal-social-behavior-and-behavioral-problems-of-domestic-animals/behavioral-problems-of-dogs.

3.   K. L. Overall. Interview by Dina Roth Port, May 29, 2018.

4.   E. Ward, "Motion Sickness in Dogs," VCA Hospitals, 2011, accessed April 2, 2018. vcahospitals.com/know-your-pet/motion-sickness-in-dogs.

5.   G. Elert, *The Physics Factbook: Frequency Range of Dog Hearing,* accessed January 25, 2018. hypertextbook.com/facts/2003/TimCondon.shtml.

CHAPTER 16: SEPARATION ANXIETY

1.   "Common Dog Behavior Issues: Separation Anxiety," American Society for the Prevention of Cruelty to Animals, accessed April 12, 2018. www.aspca.org/pet-care/dog-care/common-dog-behavior-issues/separation-anxiety.

2.   G. M. Landsberg and S. Denenberg, "Behavior Problems of Dogs," *Merck Veterinary Manual,* accessed April 1, 2018. www.merckvetmanual.com/behavior/normal-social-behavior-and-behavioral-problems-of-domestic-animals/behavioral-problems-of-dogs.

3.   "Common Dog Behavior Issues: Separation Anxiety," American Society for the Prevention of Cruelty to Animals, accessed April 12, 2018. www.aspca.org/pet-care/dog-care/common-dog-behavior-issues/separation-anxiety.

4.   S. Borns-Weil. Interview by Dina Roth Port, May 14, 2018.

5.   K. Tiira and H. Lohi, "Early Life Experiences and Exercise Associate with Canine Anxieties," *PLoS ONE* 10, no. 11 (2015).

6.   T. Rehn and L. J. Keeling, "The Effect of Time Left Alone at Home on Dog Welfare," *Applied Animal Behaviour Science* 129, no. 2–4 (2011): 129–135.

CHAPTER 17: HYPERACTIVITY

1.   U. A. Luescher, "Hyperkinesis in Dogs: Six Case Reports," *Canadian Veterinary Journal* 34, no. 6 (1993): 368–370.

2.   N. Hoppe et al., "Correlates of Attention Deficit Hyperactivity Disorder (ADHD)-Like Behavior in Domestic Dogs: First Results

from a Questionnaire-Based Study," *Veterinary Medicine* 2, no. 3, 95–118.

3. J. Ciribassi. Interview by Dina Roth Port, May 8, 2018.

4. V. Schade. "How to Calm a High-Energy Dog," petMD, accessed April 10, 2018. www.petmd.com/dog/behavior/how-calm-high-energy-dog.

CHAPTER 18: AGGRESSION

1. J. Pierce, "Understanding Aggression in Dogs," *Psychology Today,* June 14, 2012, accessed April 20, 2018. www.psychologytoday .com/us/blog/all-dogs-go-heaven/201206/understanding-aggression-in-dogs.

2. J. Hoffman, "Is This Dog Dangerous? Shelters Live with Live-or-Die Tests," *New York Times,* July 31, 2017, accessed April 20, 2018. www.nytimes.com/2017/07/31/science/dogs-shelters-adoption-behavior-tests.html.

3. T. Camps et al., "Pain-Related Aggression in Dogs: 12 Clinical Cases," *Journal of Veterinary Behavior* 7, no. 2 (2012): 99–102.

4. E. L. MacLean et al., "Endogenous Oxytocin, Vasopressin, and Aggression in Domestic Dogs," *Frontiers in Psychology* 8 (2017): 1613.

5. "Breed-Specific Policies: No Basis in Science," Humane Society of the United States, accessed April 30, 2018. www.humanesociety .org/issues/breed-specific-legislation/fact_sheets/breed-specific-legislation-no-basis-in-science.html.

6. G. J. Patronek et al.,"Co-occurrence of Potentially Preventable Factors in 256 Dog Bite-Related Fatalities in the United States (2000–2009)," *Journal of the American Veterinary Medical Association* 243, no. 12 (2013): 1726–1736.

7. L. Ragatz et al., "Vicious Dogs: The Antisocial Behaviors and Psychological Characteristics of Owners," *Journal of Forensic Sciences* 54, no. 3 (2009): 699–703; J. E. Barnes et al, "Ownership of High-Risk ("Vicious") Dogs as a Marker for Deviant Behaviors: Implications for Risk Assessment," *Journal of Interpersonal Violence* 21, no. 12 (2006): 1616–1634; R. A. Casey et al., Human Directed Aggression in Domestic Dogs (*Canis familiaris*): Occurrence in Different

Contexts and Risk Factors. *Applied Animal Behaviour Science* 152 (2014): 52–63.

8. "7 Tips on Canine Body Language," *ASPCApro*, accessed May 2, 2018. www.aspcapro.org/resource/7-tips-canine-body-language; "Common Dog Behavior Issues: Aggression," American Society for the Prevention of Cruelty to Animals, accessed May 3, 2018.

9. M. E. Herron et al., "Survey of the Use and Outcome of Confrontational and Nonconfrontational Training Methods in Client-Owned Dogs Showing Undesired Behaviors," *Applied Animal Behaviour Science* 117, no. 1–2 (2009): 47–54.

10. M. Herron. Interview by Dina Roth Port, January 26, 2015.

11. Ibid.

12. "Common Dog Behavior Issues: Food Guarding," American Society for the Prevention of Cruelty to Animals, accessed May 10, 2018. www.aspca.org/pet-care/dog-care/common-dog-behavior-issues/food-guarding.

13. S. C. Kahler, "Unmasking the Shelter Dog," *Journal of the American Veterinary Medical Association*, March 18, 2015, accessed May 12, 2018. www.avma.org/News/JAVMANews/Pages/150401a.aspx.

14. "Dog Bite Prevention," American Veterinary Medical Association, accessed May 20, 2018. www.avma.org/public/Pages/Dog-Bite-Prevention.aspx.

CHAPTER 22: NOT LISTENING WITHOUT TREATS

1. S. B. Kendall, "Preference for Intermittent Reinforcement," *Journal of the Experimental Analysis of Behavior* 21, no. 3 (1974): 463–473; R. M. Hogarth and M. C. Villeval, "Ambiguous Incentives and the Persistence of Effort: Experimental Evidence," *Journal of Economic Behavior and Organization* 100(2014): 1–19; S. Weinschenk, "Use Unpredictable Rewards to Keep Behavior Going," *Psychology Today,* November 13, 2013. www.psychologytoday.com/us/blog/brain-wise/201311/use-unpredictable-rewards-keep-behavior-going.

ABOUT THE AUTHORS

© Rachel Goyette

Zak George is a trainer who has worked with thousands of dogs since he started his career in 2004. His YouTube channel, Zak George's Dog Training Revolution, is the number one destination for video dog training content in the world, and he is the author of *Zak George's Dog Training Revolution: The Complete Guide to Raising the Perfect Pet with Love*.

Zak has starred in two of his own dog training shows, Animal Planet's *Superfetch* and the BBC's *Who Let the Dogs Out?* He has also appeared as an expert on various other Animal Planet shows such as *Dogs 101*, as well as many national talk shows and news programs such as *Late Night with David Letterman, Late Night with Jimmy Fallon, The Early Show* on CBS, *Fox and Friends*, and *Rachael Ray*.

Zak's goal is to raise the standards in the dog training industry as he advocates for the latest in scientific understanding of dog behavior while balancing this approach with twenty-first-century ethics. He also heavily emphasizes the importance of prioritizing the relationship with our dogs in order to achieve incredible results.

Zak lives in New Orleans with his wife, Bree; their dog, Indiana; and their cat, Angela.

© Larry Port

Dina Roth Port is an award-winning journalist, coauthor of *Zak George's Dog Training Revolution: The Complete Guide to Raising the Perfect Pet with Love*, and author of *Previvors: Facing the Breast Cancer Gene and Making Life-Changing Decisions*.

She launched her freelance writing career in 2002, and since then her articles have appeared in dozens of print and online publications such as *Glamour, Self, Prevention, Fitness, Cosmopolitan, Parenting*, Parents.com, the *Huffington Post*, Intel.com, and WebMD. A graduate of Northwestern University's Medill School of Journalism, Dina has also worked as an editor at *Glamour* and *Parenting* magazines, and she is the director of content at Rocket Matter, a cloud-based legal software company.

Dina lives in Boca Raton, Florida, with her husband, Larry, and their two children. Of course, her family wouldn't be complete without their beloved pets: Baxter, Brody, and Kitty Cupcake.

INDEX

OCD, 130
off-leash training, 184–91
Ostojić, Ljerka, 34
outside-in training, 15–17
Overall, Karen L., 40, 130

P

patience, importance of, 30–31
people
    aggressive behavior toward,
        169–70
    fear of, 135–38
    jumping on, 70–75
    resource guarding of, 160–63
phobias
    definition of, 124
    fear vs., 124
    noise, 132–35
    See also anxiety; fear
places, fear of, 127–28
play
    as currency, 21–22
    importance of, 8
play biting
    dealing with, 76, 78–82
    reasons for, 77
poop, eating
    dealing with, 116–18
    reasons for, 115–16
potty problems
    dealing with, 83, 84–89
    reasons for, 84, 87–88, 89
praise, 20, 193
primary training, 23–24
prong collars, 4, 15–16, 20, 30,
    99, 157

punishment
    definition of, 19–20
    physical, 20
puppies
    chewing by, 67, 68
    controlling environment for, 18
    digging by, 111, 112–13
    exercise for, 14
    mouthing by, 76, 77
    socialization and, 42–43, 125
pushy behaviors, 100–104

R

reinforcement
    currency and, 20–23
    definition of, 19
    intermittent, 22
    rate of, 193–96
relationship, prioritizing, 7–9
resource guarding, 160–63
running away, 190–91

S

secondary training, 24–25
Seligman, Martin, 30
separation anxiety
    barking and, 58, 62–63
    dealing with, 143–46
    prevalence of, 142
    reasons for, 142–43
    signs of, 141–42
"settle," teaching, 101–3
shock collars. *See* electric shock
        collars
"sit," teaching, 46

Published in the United States by Ten Speed Press, an imprint of
Random House, a division of Penguin Random House LLC, New York.
www.crownpublishing.com
www.tenspeed.com

Ten Speed Press and the Ten Speed Press colophon are registered
trademarks of Penguin Random House LLC.

Library of Congress Cataloging-in-Publication Data
Names: George, Zak, author.
Title: Zak George's guide to a well-behaved dog : proven solutions to
   the most common training problems for all ages, breeds, and mixes /
   by Zak George with Dina Roth Port.
Other titles: Guide to a well-behaved dog
Description: First edition. | New York : Ten Speed Press, an imprint of the
   Crown Publishing Group, [2019] | Includes bibliographical references
   and index.
Identifiers: LCCN 2019008706)
Subjects: LCSH: Dogs—Training.
Classification: LCC SF431 .G434 2019 | DDC 636.7/0835—dc23 LC
   record available at https://lccn.loc.gov/2019008706

Trade Paperback ISBN: 978-0-399-58241-7
eBook ISBN: 978-0-399-58242-4

Printed in the United States of America.

Front cover photograph by Daymon Gardner
Design by Leona Chelsea Legarte

10 9 8 7 6

First Edition